The Unholy War:

Israel and Palestine
1897-1971

The Unholy War:

Israel and Palestine
1897-1971

David Waines

Foreword by Maxime Rodinson

MEDINA UNIVERSITY PRESS INTERNATIONAL

Wilmette, Illinois

First published in the United States by
The Medina University Press International
908 Ashland Avenue
Wilmette, Illinois   60091
1971

ISBN 0-88870-001-6
LIBRARY OF CONGRESS CATALOGUE CARD NUMBER 70-148-171

Legal Deposit, 1st Quarter 1971
Quebec National Library

Printed in Canada

TO
THE TRIUMVIRATE:
N.H.O.
D.L.W.
W.J.W.

9

Table of Contents

Foreword

It seems almost redundant to introduce David Waines' book. THE UNHOLY WAR is a book that speaks for itself. It is honest, frank, direct and sensitive. It does not seek to conceal the painful ambiguities of reality behind a camouflage of intolerant slogans.

The honesty of this work will be contested only by those whose minds are shuttered by a narrow ideological perspective, by those who emotionally deny the slightest possibility of truth in a version of the past which differs from the one instilled in them and which has molded their concepts of love, hatred and fear. The walls which surround, confine and block the thoughts of such people can only be shattered by a calamity touching them to the very depths of their being. The very least a book like this can do is pave the way for the breakup of old and false convictions. It can set off the first liberating spark of doubt. At the same time it will convince open minds receptive to truth.

The author is an historian accustomed to the use of basic historical material. His documentation is flawless. He clearly knows how to weigh the relative value of evidence and to draw conclusions as fairly as human weakness permits. Moreover, he has taken a leap forward in historical perspective. Although specialized in medieval Middle Eastern history, he felt, and quite rightly, that the contemporary Arabs merit at least as much concern as the Arabs of bygone eras. He also felt that the rules for a critical understanding of facts as applied to the past can equally be applied to current events. THE UNHOLY WAR is well researched and carefully documented, particularly for the period of the British Mandate in Palestine, a period of crucial importance in which all the signs of a grim future can be discerned.

In addition, he has aptly elucidated his account with anecdotes of personal contacts with the men and women involved, and the things they told him. How often the spoken word reveals the depth of problems better than many pages of detailed narrative! I, for one, am well aware of the pitfalls involved in this approach, but these are outweighed by the advantages of direct contact with day-to-day reality and the chance to pursue an investigation more thoroughly without being restricted by scanty documentary evidence. It is preferable by far to follow this path than to allow oneself to reach fatuous, uncritical judgments based only on impressions and passions.

Let me now try to extract the core of the author's argument as I understand it. And permit me to add, *en passant,* that I share his interpretation.

David Waines uses as his starting point a simple premise, but one that is all too often neglected. The Arabs, and the Palestinians in particular, are human beings. As such their human and political behavior may be criticized; indeed, on many points it must be criticized. Nevertheless, it is a behavior which is intelligible because it results from a particular situation and not from some inherent wickedness of the Arabs themselves. And by thus "explaining" Arab behavior, I do not mean that it should be "glorified." On the contrary, what is required is to tear off the mask of invective worn by so many in the West through which the Arabs' behavior is viewed as utterly unintelligible and irrational, and which is therefore fit only to be reviled and castigated.

We must go a step further. For example, one might argue that in the context of history the Hitler phenomenon can be explained. So it can. But sanity demands that one should add that Hitler's options were criminal in principle because they envisaged, without hesitation, the destruction of the individual and the annihilation of the innocent even before that of the enemy. Confronted by the critical situation in Germany in the nineteen-thirties, other options, humane options, were possible.

Let us admit that in certain Arab circles inhumane options are pursued. However, their protest against Zionist and Israeli usurpation is, in itself, a normal reaction, a defense any other people would resort to in the same circumstances. From the very beginning, the Palestinians were the ones militated against. Yet this is precisely what ill-informed Zionist and pro-Israeli Western opinion rejects. For them, the very fact of the Arab protest is criminal. That it is *not* criminal in itself is a simple fact, but an essential one.

Another aspect of the same theme has already been alluded

to. This is the need to shake the self-complacent conscience of the West, including that of the Jew. *"Une bonne conscience est un doux oreiller,"* says a French proverb. "An easy, tranquil conscience is a soft pillow." On a soft pillow one sleeps well. One is blinded by one's own thoughts and aspirations and those of his own people. One sees neither the sufferings caused to others, nor the defeat inflicted on truth and justice. It is easy to justify the most detestable of our acts in order to preserve this cosy refuge. Since we are essentially good and just, everything that safeguards us is good. Like a befuddled mind, a lazy conscience creates monsters.

The West has grave responsibilities to bear in the drama of the Palestinians and Jews alike. It is all too easy to wash one's hands of responsibility toward one people while giving free rein to the other. It is also easy to leave two victimized peoples — one of which has, in addition, become the victim of the other — to unravel their own problems. We all have a pressing obligation toward this dreadful problem which was created and aggravated, with our tacit complicity, by the political leaders of the West.

The case of the Jews is more difficult still. I use the word "Jews" in its broadest sense, that is, to embrace all those who have been put in the same position as the Jews, some because of their religion or culture and others, like myself, because of a vestige of cultural attitudes by which one is indirectly associated through ancestry or directly through ancestry itself. The Jews have been victims, victims of Christian society, victims also (but more sporadically and in a much less intense and systematic fashion) of Muslim society, victims of many political, economic, social and ideological attitudes and programs. It's the fate one could expect for a minority group such as the Jews. None of this stems from a particular malediction. It can be explained, although this makes it nonetheless condemnable. As a result it becomes the duty of men of goodwill everywhere to denounce any and every form of persecution aimed at Jews as such, and to eradicate all traces and effects of the position of inferiority, contempt and humiliation in which they have been placed for centuries. To me this is self-evident and indisputable.

It is normal, but equally deplorable, that this same situation has developed a self-righteous conscience among many Jews. Those

who have condemned their humiliation and persecution have
developed, in addition, a kind of secondary complacent conscience
which, if I may say so, attributes to Jews an impeccability
belonging only to gods.

It is not a question, as Aristotle put it, of beasts or gods. We
are dealing with flesh and blood human beings; their tenure as
victims, durable though it may have been, is not enough to
erase their human characteristics. Men — even the oppressed of
yesterday — are, unfortunately, capable of becoming the oppressors of tomorrow.

This has come to pass with certain Jews and especially with
Zionist Jews. Even if certain Arabs, by their nature, have the
tendency to indict the very souls of these same Jews, it is not
a question here of condemning them to everlasting hell and
damnation. Their behavior can also be explained. It is the
behavior of men, not of monsters. Any people in their situation
would probably have followed the same road. The most prominent
factors underlying their motivation are something more than
sheer malevolence. They are ignorance and blind ideology.
Absolute necessity compelled some, completely innocent, to align
themselves with others. For many adherents of the Zionist
ideology, but not for all, other options, more generous and
intelligent, were possible.

The Arabs are not a sacred people, neither are the Jews.
Thus, it is one thing to explain the chain of events that led to
the Zionist solution, to show its human and non-demonic
dimensions, to relate this solution to ultimate responsibilities
which are not Jewish — that is, the responsibility of Christian
society in particular. However, it is quite another thing to blind
oneself to reality, to speak of historical rights which, upon the
slightest reflection, are shown to be mere fantasy, to justify all
the steps taken by the Zionist leaders — whose movement is
capable of the same aberrations of any ideological movement — to
pretend that somehow, miraculously, the establishment of a
Jewish state on Arab soil could be accomplished by means
other than the subordination or expulsion of the indigenous
population. There are still others who insist that, no less
miraculously, the behavior of Israelis is constantly angelic, who
justify all this by conversely attributing to the Arabs a demonic

nature, thus striking down with reproach any protest raised against an injustice committed by one Jew or a group of Jews.

And the self-righteous Arab conscience?, one asks. It is often exasperating. It too needs to be shaken to show that Arabs are as capable as others of committing oppressive acts and to demonstrate that because a society is Arab (or Jewish) does not ensure it against irrational and unjust decisions. Pro-Arab sentimentalists and ideologists — like pro-Jews of the same type — have a tendency to reach conclusions of this kind.

David Waines avoids the pitfall of following this line of reasoning. He does not hide what should be criticized in the actions of certain Arabs. I, too, do not conceal that the plan of procedure, the strategy and tactics of certain Palestinian organizations are far from being above reproach. One can and must reproach Arabs, even those among them who play to the hilt the role of victim which, for ages, has been that of the Jews and which is still theirs in certain countries. This right of criticism, however, belongs only to those who face the fact that the Zionist movement has caused the Palestinians fundamental and undeserved harm. Otherwise, one is either blind or partisan.

The path of true and fair judgment has never been an easy one. The problem with which this book deals is particularly thorny and the road is especially narrow and difficult lying, as it does, between the two precipices of a fundamentalist and rigid Arabophobia and Judeophobia to each of which, ironically, is ascribed the common term of anti-Semitism. It seems to me that David Waines has known how to follow this difficult road with extraordinary fairness. The reader will easily be able to judge for himself.

Maxime Rodinson,
Sorbonne, Paris.

Prologue

All too often we assume that our first awareness of a problem is indicative of the time it came into being. This was the position I found myself in when I went to the Sudan in 1957 as a student. I was already an "armchair politician" and, like most North Americans, I knew at least a little about the hard-working band of pioneers who, led by David Ben Gurion, had created Israel as a model democratic state amid the backwardness and poverty of the Arab Middle East. The Suez crisis was just over, and like most in the West I admired the skill and tenacity of the young Israeli Army.

It is, of course, no fault of the armchair politician that his analysis of a current international problem must be based on the information available in daily newspapers or on the television news where he can see the replay action of a battle which may have occurred only hours before in some far away, instant graveyard.

An example is the Arab-Israeli War of June 1967. Television cameramen followed the battle across the empty wastes of the Sinai Desert and up the slopes of the Golan Heights. The Security Council debates on the crisis were telecast live and seemed to place us right in the heart of international diplomacy. How long will it be before the roving cameraman in the United Nations also captures on film the drama of political arm-twisting in the corridors? The magazines too had their function, providing "in depth" analyses of the causes and significance of the crisis as well as background sketches of some of the leading characters, including the now-deceased President Gamal Abdel Nasser, General Moshe Dayan and Ahmad Shukayri.

We were then bombarded with a flood of "instant" books on the war. Incredible as it may seem, the first one appeared only days after the battle had ended! Other, more thoughtful books followed, skillfully dissecting the war hour by hour. This massive output of analysis and opinion could have provided a clearer understanding of the entire Arab-Israeli conflict. Instead, it produced an ever more confusing and perplexing picture of the situation.

It is important to know why this is so. In the first place, the
June war was not seen in its historical context. It is understandable that limitations of time and space in the television and newspaper coverage did not permit a reflective backward glance to
the very roots of the conflict. The "instant" books made the same
omissions.

The basic causes of the June war are not to be found in the
weeks immediately prior to the crisis. The causes lie partly in
the aftermath of the Suez crisis of 1956 when Britain, France
and Israel invaded Egypt, and partly in the Arab-Israeli War of
1948 which followed the creation of the State of Israel. It may
well be that an enduring solution to the Arab-Israeli dilemma
will not be found by turning the clock back to May 1967, to 1956
or even to 1948. To *understand* the problem, we must revert to
its basic roots.

This leads to a second point, a subtle but important difference
in terminology. In North America we speak of the Arab-Israeli
conflict. In the Arab world they speak only of the Palestine Problem. This does not mean that the Arabs generally disclaim interest
in the conflict. Far from it. It means rather that the core of the
problem is viewed from a different perspective.

In any bitter controversy each side believes it holds a
monopoly on the truth. This is human and understandable. In each
subjective argument there is an element of objective truth which
gives substance to the interpretation of each side.

For example, my Sudanese friends at the University of
Khartoum were vexed by my attitude over Suez (naïve, they
called it), and I was puzzled by theirs. One explained to me that
the crisis was a conspiracy between British and French imperialism
and their Israeli protégé. The British wanted to repossess the
Suez Canal, the French wanted to overthrow Nasser because of
his assistance to the Algerians rebelling against the tyranny of
French rule, and Israel was bent upon another reckless adventure
of expansion. I didn't see the crisis in that light at all. Besides,
the idea of a conspiracy seemed quite ludicrous and why would
Israel want to expand into the Sinai Desert of all places?

It mattered little that time would prove my friends substantially
correct. It is now accepted that a conspiracy did exist between the
three invading powers. Even Prime Minister Ben Gurion had at

the time claimed before the Israeli Parliament that, by attacking Sinai, Israel had not invaded *Egypt proper*, but had merely *liberated* part of the ancient Jewish homeland. Nevertheless, the confrontation revealed to me that not only could divergent views be held concerning the same events, but also that these views could be voiced with a deep conviction because these things mattered in their lives. When a Sudanese student spoke to me of imperialism and colonialism, he was reminding me that Britain had only recently relinquished her rule over his country. That was an experience in which I had had no share and I could not then grasp the fine combination of intellectual appraisal and emotional involvement.

From the Arab perspective the Palestine Problem is simply the displacement of the inhabitants of Palestine under conditions of British colonial rule by another people, Zionists, who were fired with a political ideology which threatened the status of the Arab community. After 1948 and the creation of the State of Israel, the conflict remained essentially "the struggle of an indigenous population against the occupation of part of its normal territory by foreigners."[1] This is the substance of the Arab position, and it is cast strictly in terms of the fate and the struggle of the people of Palestine. All other elements of the broader Arab-Israeli conflict stem from this. But again, faced as we are with the half-real world of the news media and the effects of time and distance on our powers of perception, the subjective interpretation of the Palestinian case has become distorted and unreal. The consequence is that even the substance of their story has been kicked into oblivion.

Nevertheless, Palestinians are what the problem is all about. And this book is about the problem of Palestine.

The Sudan was a good place to begin one's education on the Middle East. Jordan 1962 was a good place to continue. In the summer of that year, I had intended merely to spend a leisurely six-week vacation in Lebanon, Syria and Jordan. But 1962 was a year of dramatic upheaval. Caught there as a bystander I was

[1] *Israel and the Arabs* by Maxime Rodinson, Penguin Special, London (1968).

soon swept into the maelstrom of events causing me to prolong
my stay well into 1963. The Royalist Regime in Yemen had just
been toppled by the Republicans, who had chased the royal head
of state and his tribesmen north into the inaccessible mountains.
Iraq witnessed a coup d'etat, and I myself nearly witnessed one
in Damascus which I had left scarcely two days earlier.

It was in Jordan, however, that the greatest tension seemed to
be concentrated. Everywhere one encountered Palestinians, that
embittered remnant of a people who had once inhabited the land
now known as Israel. At that time they made up more than half
of King Hussein's kingdom and represented a potential threat
to both his person and his throne. The relationship between the
king and the Palestinians was an odd love-hate affair. He bore
the stigma of his grandfather's "betrayal" when, after the 1948
war, King Abdullah had tried to make a deal with the Israelis.
His efforts cost him his life; he was assassinated by a Palestinian
youth in a Jerusalem mosque. King Hussein could expect no
less were he to follow on the same path. On the other hand,
he was regarded as a courageous and modest ruler. His country
was not inherently wealthy like several of the oil kingdoms,
but he had nursed and pushed it toward economic viability.
Though the ultimate authority in his kindgom, he was not aloof
like most monarchs. Often he would visit his ministers in their
homes and he could be seen driving his own car through the
streets of Amman.

When I first arrived in Amman I was exhausted. It had been
a seven-hour car trip from Beirut, across the mountains down to
the shimmering garden city of Damascus, and then through the
stifling mid-afternoon heat to Amman. A Jordanian border guard
had suggested a hotel in Amman where he told our taxi driver
to leave me. It was clean and cool and after a shower I went in
search of a good meal. I was too shy to speak Arabic except with
those who, I was sure, did not understand English.

This is how it came about that as I was haltingly asking a
porter about a restaurant two boys, who looked like students,
approached me, one saying: *"Ta' ma'na, badna nakul kamaan."*
(Come with us, we too are going to eat.)

"Shukran," I replied and followed them toward the door.

"You're American," the one said pleasantly, in English.

"Canadian," I politely corrected him, noting ruefully how quickly he had spotted my appalling accent.

"You speak Arabic very well," he said. Relieved by his generosity, I confessed he had come along just as I was running out of appropriate phrases with the porter. The ice was broken and I spent the rest of the evening with Khalil and Jelal.

When we stepped into the street the sun had already gone down and a cool breeze was blowing in from the desert. The restaurant was some distance from the hotel and, as we walked, I learned that my companions were students in the Faculty of Engineering at the American University of Beirut. They had come to Amman to visit friends for the weekend. Both were tall and lean, dark of complexion and each spoke with a quiet intensity and purpose, but not without humor, as I soon learned.

The restaurant they chose was called Ali Baba. Inside it looked like an oriental rogues' gallery with imaginative portraits of the forty thieves spaced at intervals around the walls. The picture of Ali Baba hung in the place of honor above the doorway.

"You know the tale of Ali Baba and his gang of thieves," said Jelal. Of course. What child has not read the Tales of the Arabian Nights with Ali Baba and Aladdin and his magic lamp?

"How many thieves were in the band?" asked Khalil, smiling quietly.

"Forty," I replied without hesitation.

This aroused their glee and they told me to count the portraits. I had counted down one wall when I noticed something out of context — on the back wall of the restaurant, in a space slightly above and between two of the thieves, I spotted a different picture. Whether out of malice or respect, I know not, the proprietor had placed a framed photograph of the king, making him a so-called forty-first "thief." This is when I realized that my companions must be Palestinians.

Their story was simple. Khalil, the son of a minor official of the Palestinian Government, was born in Jaffa and Jelal, a doctor's son, in Haifa. The boys were about eight years old when their families were forced to flee from the terrors of the war in 1948. These two families were more fortunate than hundreds of thousands of their countrymen who had spent the years since the war in refugee camps. Khalil's father found employment in a ministry of the Jordanian Government, and Jelal's father was able to set up a medical practice in Amman even though he had lost all the land his family had owned near Haifa. Fate had brought Khalil and Jelal to the same school in Amman and now they were on Point-4 American Government Aid Scholarships at the American University in Beirut.

Our conversation was to the point: a capsule of the Palestine Problem.

"Why did you choose your particular line of study, and what of the future?" I asked them.

"One day Palestine will need professional men and engineers will be called upon to help build that future."

"But you live in Jordan now. Is this not your country?"

"We live in Jordan, it's true, but Palestine is our home as it has been our fathers' and their fathers' before them."

My next question was: "How do you expect to go back to your home, to Palestine, or rather to Israel?"

"One day the world will acknowledge the injustice done to our people, and we shall return."

This was their fundamental article of faith: "We shall return." Never again did I see Jelal or Khalil after that night in Amman.

From the capital I traveled the length of the West Bank of Jordan. Strange places soon became familiar: Tulkarm, Nablus, Ramallah. The well-known names of Jerusalem, Hebron, Jericho and Bethlehem assumed an altogether different reality for me from the images of these ancient places which I had retained since childhood. Wherever I talked with Palestinians, whether in a coffee shop in Jerusalem, a schoolroom in Tulkarm, a private home in Nablus or a refugee camp in Jericho, I heard the same phrase: "We shall return." It echoed down the rocky hills and through the green valleys.

Their poets too, even the least among them, tried to capture the sense of loss which sustained the passion for their return. These are the words of a native of Jaffa, an exile gazing from a height of land on the West Bank toward the gray expanse of the Mediterranean he had once known so well:

Wounded shore! Vainly fluttering before my eyes!
You are ever in my heart.
Not in humiliation will I return,
Will you, liberated, welcome me back?
My hands outstretched to you
Fall wearily beneath the weight of longing.
When I weep, lamenting my loss
I weep for myself and you.

These words came back to me as I again sat in the gracious lounge of the Grand Hotel in Ramallah. Five years had passed. It was September 1967, two months after the Six Day War and Ramallah, like the entire West Bank of Jordan, was occupied by the Israeli Army. The man who had written the above lines sat across from me. Kamal Nasser was perhaps forty, with thinning black hair, a tanned face and deep brown eyes which animated his conversation as he endlessly lit one cigarette after another. He had led an active life on the Jordanian political scene, in journalism, in parliament and in prison. He spoke softly and intensely of the Arab defeat.

"We have been humiliated by this disaster. The morale of our people has been shattered, and yet we shall pick up the pieces and begin again. The Arab leaders have let us down, Nasser, Hussein and the rest. Our faith in the United Nations' ability to solve this problem has been misplaced; perhaps we were too naïve in believing in its power. Now we shall have to fall back upon our own resources; we shall resist the Israeli occupation peacefully as long as we can, in whatever form we can. But somehow I believe that this is what Winston Churchill once said — not the end, nor the beginning of the end, but rather the end of the beginning. The beginning of the revival of our people, the Palestinians." That was Kamal Nasser in 1967. Today, after his expulsion by the Israelis from the West Bank, he is one of the political leaders of Fateh.

Time will tell whether the Palestinians are at the beginning of the end or the end of the beginning. In any event, the Six Day War and the Israeli occupation of the West Bank (formerly part of Palestine), have brought the Palestinians back to center stage. In the past, their script was written by other hands. This is not

likely to happen in the future. As Yassir Arafat said just
before civil war erupted in Jordan: "Everyone wants to sweep
the Palestinians under the rug. But we are not dust yet."

Arafat's comment brings us back to the subject of this book,
the chronic and unholy war for that piece of land which three
religious faiths claim to be holy, and which two claim to be
theirs alone. Since the late nineteenth century, the "unholy war"
has really been a war between two nationalisms: Zionist and
Arab. In recent years there has been a further crystallization.
The decisive struggle has resolved itself to being a very ancient
struggle in terms of faith, but also a very modern one on the part
of guerillas against the most recent and efficient weaponry. It is
a modern battle in an ancient setting. And while the Zionist
and Arab worlds are active bystanders who became involved at
crucial points in this war — really the Fifty Years' War —
the everyday war is the one that is fought between Israel and
Palestine. It is this war and its background which is the concern
of this book.

1

"A People Without a Land..."

One version has it that the Six Day War of June 1967 began in 1897, the year Theodore Herzl founded the World Zionist Organization. Zionism however, at least in the abstract, initially had nothing to do with either the Arabs or the Middle East. Zionists were preoccupied with the growing menace of anti-Semitism on the Continent, a disease which had reached alarming proportions during the last quarter of the nineteenth century.

European imperialism, which had already afflicted the Middle East for some time, would continue to be a painful reality to the peoples of the Arab world. France achieved a foothold in North Africa by seizing Algeria in the eighteen-thirties, and then Tunisia in 1881. In 1882 Great Britain "temporarily" occupied Egypt to secure the Suez Canal, that vital artery of the imperial lifeline joining Britain to Gibraltar, Malta, Cyprus, Aden and thence to India. The occupation did not end completely until King Farouk's overthrow in 1952.

Between Herzl's 1897 activities and the end of World War I, Zionist nationalist ideals had forged a bond of common purpose with the imperial strategy of the British Government. The attention of each was focused on Palestine. The bond which linked their purpose was the Balfour Declaration. Issued in November 1917, the declaration was as momentous a document as the idea which inspired it. When Zionists brought to England their incredible scheme for the solution of "the Jewish problem," a Jewish national home, the outcome was highly speculative. No one could have foreseen the irony that was to unfold: the eve of the fiftieth anniversary of the Balfour Declaration occurred in the very year that Zionism's child, the State of Israel, was again at war with the Arabs. At the same time the last outpost of the British Empire in the Middle East was being abandoned in Aden. British imperialism died ungracefully, but the Palestine Problem remains a dangerous issue.

The story begins with the rise of Zionism in the late nineteenth century as an answer to the secular problem of anti-Semitism which itself was a product of European Christianity. Hatred of the Jew had for centuries been a part of Church propaganda and, although not effective everywhere, it did reach the highest ranks of the clergy. Men such as St. John Chrysostom, St. Bernard and Peter the Venerable count among those who had added their voice to the traditional Christian indictment of the Jew for the death of Christ. To kill a Jew in the twelfth century was regarded as a virtue — an excess of virtue. Peter the Venerable once said: "God does not wish to annihilate the Jew. He must be made to suffer fearful torments, and be preserved for greater ignominy, for an existence more bitter than death." The Jew was despised as the living symbol of God's wrath for his crime of deicide. Christianity's rationalization of the persecution of the Jew evolved over the centuries into a social and political persecution based on racial theories.

During the nineteenth century, in the wake of the liberalizing spirit of the French Revolution, the Jew in Western Europe found himself emancipated from centuries of bondage, and allowed to become an assimilated member of the country he inhabited. Nevertheless, modern or political anti-Semitism derived in the same century from persons who saw in the Jewish emancipation all that was offensive in the liberal revolutionary movements. It was believed that the Jews were a people apart — a people who did not belong as full participants of European society.

The Western European Jews who continued to struggle against these currents were firmly convinced that the final answer to "the Jewish problem" lay in their genuine freedom and assimilation within their own society be it French, English, or German.

In Central and Eastern Europe, on the other hand, the ideas of emancipation were not to take root. No practical improvement had occurred in the medieval condition of urban Jewish ghettos. The impoverished rural townlets within the Pale of Settlement, that prison house created by czarist Russia for the majority of its Jewish inhabitants, fared little better. In these Jewish communities spiritual sustenance compensated somehow (if anything could) for physical privation. But when Czar Alexander II fell victim to an assassin's bullet there was no refuge, even in prayer, from the officially inspired torrent of violence and terror which marked Russian vengeance against an alleged Jewish conspiracy. Anti-Jewish pogroms swept over Russia on an unprecedented scale. Pogroms were a sadly familiar part of Russian Jewish life. Odessa during Easter of 1871 had been the scene of the worst outbreak in recent memory, but 1881 was a year of crisis for many Jews. The extent of the violence — nearly 150 cities and villages witnessed pogroms — and the fact that the usual illiterate rabble was now supported by men of status, including government officials, added a new dimension to the horror.

Mobs, like packs of ravenous wolves, stormed and pillaged Jewish shops, homes, schools and synagogues. The press stoked the fires of hatred with horrendous accounts of every imaginable sin, deceit and wickedness ascribed to Jews. Books were written to prove that Jews drank the blood of Christian children. In this cauldron of fear and hate the venom of man's unreason boiled over.

The new wave of repression was officially marked by the so-called May Laws of 1882 of which Chaim Weizmann later wrote: "It seemed that the whole cumbersome machinery of the vast Russian Empire was created for the sole purpose of inventing and amplifying rules and regulations for the hedging in of the existence of its Jewish subjects until it became something that was neither life nor death."

The very year of the infamous May Laws saw the appearance of another document in which one Russian Jew, Leo Pinsker, penned his response to the terrible dilemma of his people. In a small pamphlet entitled *Auto-Emancipation*,[11] Pinsker stated that the Jews must emancipate themselves from their political disabilities, establishing for themselves a nation with all the usual attributes: a common language, common customs and a common land from which no foreign master could expel them. Although he considered Palestine a reasonable location, Pinsker was more conscious of articulating the dangers inherent in Jewish minority status anywhere in the world. The national home, therefore, "might form a small territory in North America, or a sovereign *pashalik* in Asiatic Turkey recognized by the Porte and the other Powers as neutral." It was the first coherent and reasoned statement for the rebirth of Zion.

Two alternatives to the Jews' position seemed possible. The Jew of Western Europe saw his solution in assimilation as an equal member of his own society. The idea of a Jewish nation might be repugnant to him, for he regarded Jews as sharing only their religion in common. The Jew of Eastern Europe seized upon the nationalist ideal by which he would mold his own destiny within a Jewish nation dependent upon no one but himself.

The specific form of the Jewish problem which Zionism emerged to resolve was the ghetto life in Russia and Eastern Europe. Zionists therefore championed Jewish nationalism and at the same time rejected the efforts of the western Jew to assimilate within Gentile society, or to be emancipated on Gentile terms.

The founder of the Zionist movement, Theodore Herzl (1860-1904) summed up the aim and motivation of Jewish nationalism in these words: "Let the sovereignty be granted us over a portion of the globe large enough to satisfy the rightful requirements of a nation; the rest we shall manage ourselves."

Herzl, a Hungarian Jew educated in Vienna, was a lawyer by training and a journalist by profession. His impressive face was set off by piercing eyes and a fine nose; a black beard, which tumbled from his cheeks onto his chest, seemed almost to precede him as he walked. In 1891 he was appointed Paris correspondent of the Vienna newspaper, the *Neue Freie Presse*. For some years he had been concerned with the Jewish question and anti-Semitism. In 1894, while covering the famous trial of a Jewish officer of the French Army, Alfred Dreyfus, he was appalled by the overt anti-Semitism which it stirred up. The experience compelled him to compose during the following summer *Der Judenstat* (The Jewish State), the first major formulation of the Zionist thesis.[2]

In one week of feverish, anguished writing Herzl produced his ideas for the Jewish State. Unaware that Pinsker had anticipated him, especially with regard to the concept of the Jewish State, Herzl's own work was nevertheless more detailed and daring than his predecessor's. He was convinced that anti-Semitism anywhere, in any form, was an immutable force which the Jews could learn to use to their own advantage. For the Jewish masses the solution to the Jewish question must be a national one; the Jews as one people must possess their own land as a nation.

Like Pinsker, Herzl was at first vague about the precise global location of the Jewish state. In *Der Judenstat* he mentions both Argentina and Palestine as possible sites. Initially the motivation to a "return to Zion" played only a small role in the minds of early Zionists. They were more strongly imbued with the spirit and concepts of European nationalism of the late nineteenth century than the traditional Jewish ideals of the return from exile to the Holy Land. Zionism was the secularization of the Jewish messianic ideal of the redemption as a confrontation between man and God. Professor A.R. Taylor observes in his *Prelude to Israel* that "in their search for the support of all Jews, the Zionists employed the romantic idea of the 'return', a concept which holds emotional appeal for all Jews. It was thus that Zionism became mistakenly confused with Judaism, but this did not alter the essentially secular character of the Zionist movement."[3] Zionism was the Jewish quest for a kingdom in this world and was viewed as the confrontation between the Jew and the world, specifically the Gentile world. And this world, as Herzl shrewdly perceived, held the keys to that kingdom.

Herzl insisted that the first step toward the attainment of Jewish sovereignty was to secure international recognition of the Jews' right to colonize some "neutral piece of land" which could be developed, without let or hindrance, into the Jewish state. He argued that it would be fruitless to infiltrate immigrants into a particular land, for the process would continue only until "the inevitable moment when the native population feels itself threatened" and protests against further immigration. "Immigration," concluded Herzl, "is consequently futile unless based upon an assured supremacy."

Herzl immediately anticipated and then quickly ignored the one major obstacle confronting the successful creation of the Jewish state. He was aware that this "neutral" land would possess an indigenous population which might oppose the mass immigration of Jews. The potential threat of native resistance would therefore be overcome by an "assured supremacy" guaranteed the Zionists by one or more European powers.

This is the only reference in Herzl's work to a native population; nevertheless, it is important. Herzl was no longer groping
with the problem of the Jew and anti-Semite alone. A third party,
unobtrusively, had become involved. Herzl pondered the question
at the very time he was writing *The Jewish State*. In his diary
he observed that should Palestine one day become the Jewish
state it would be necessary to spirit the penniless population
across the frontier by denying it employment.[4]

This crude response to the "native problem" reflected Herzl's
simplistic view of his European environment. "The universality
with which Herzl applied his concept of anti-Semitism to all
non-Jewish peoples made it impossible from the very beginning
for the Zionists to seek truly loyal allies," Dr. Hanna Arendt has
written. "His notion of reality as an eternal, unchanging, hostile
structure — all *goyim* [Gentiles] everlastingly against all Jews —
made the identification of hard-boiledness with realism plausible
because it rendered any empirical analysis of actual political
factors seemingly superfluous."[5]

Most Zionists after Herzl shared his point of view. Their
failure to dispense with, or even alter, this basically irrational
proposition was a precipitating factor of conflict when that proposition was applied to the situation in Palestine. If, for example,
the Arab were *a priori* part of a hostile environment, then genuine
cooperation and understanding between Arab and Jew would
become impossible or, at best, exceedingly difficult. Since the
Arabs' assumed hostility could not be turned to advantage as
anti-Jewish sentiment in Europe could, then the Arab simply
had to be excluded. Herzl was not a prophet, but his words
were later to be tragically mirrored in certain Zionist activities
in Palestine when all Arab labor was excluded from Jewish-
owned land and enterprises.

Herzl's greatest contribution to Zionism lay less in his literary
output than in the demonic energy he poured into the World
Zionist Organization of which he was the founder and first pres-
ident. In August 1897, he convened a congress of Zionists in
Basle, Switzerland. In the intervening years between writing
The Jewish State and the Basle Congress he had become convinced,
largely through his contacts with Jewry in Eastern Europe, that
Palestine must become *the* site of the Jewish State. Because of

this the Congress determined the aim of Zionism to be "to create for the Jewish people a home in Palestine secured by public law." The official program was set out in four points:

1) The promotion of Jewish colonization of Palestine by Jewish agricultural and industrial workers;

2) The establishment of an organization to bind world Jewry by means of institutions in each country inhabited by Jews;

3) The strengthening of Jewish national sentiment;

4) The acquisition of government consent to the attainment of Zionist aims.

Herzl had used the word "state," the Congress the word "home" in deference to the objections of many Jews to the idea of a Jewish nation. Herzl expressed himself untroubled by semantics since he assumed devoted Zionists would in any case read "state" for "home."

The rest of Herzl's life was spent trying to obtain his international charter of recognition for the Zionist program. He may have been aware that death was stalking him (he died prematurely in 1904) as he journeyed frantically across Europe to the Middle East cajoling heads of states and empires alike to lend their support. His approaches to German Kaiser Wilhelm II and Sultan Abdul Hamid of Turkey earned him only discreet courtesies from the one, and a decoration (second class) — in some obscure Ottoman order — from the other. After these unsuccessful efforts he entered into negotiations with the British Government.

Herzl had given some thought also to the strategic importance of Palestine in the event that Britain might one day be forced from her occupation of Egypt. In his diary he wrote: "[the English] would then be obliged to seek out another road to India in place of the Suez Canal, which would then be lost to them, or at least rendered insecure. In that event a modern Jewish Palestine would resolve their difficulty."[6]

Palestine was not available for Jewish colonization when Herzl commenced his negotiations with British Foreign Secretary Joseph Chamberlain in 1903, and so he suggested that Cyprus, al-Arish and the Sinai Peninsula be granted to the Zionists. He believed that these areas could be used by the Jewish people as a rallying point in the vicinity of Palestine, which could then, in time, be taken by force.

Chamberlain listened patiently to his guest who must have appeared as a Jewish version of Cecil Rhodes, an imperialist giant whom Herzl greatly admired. Rhodes' own last words in fact would have made a fitting epitaph for Herzl: "So little done, so much to do." Chamberlain, however, was not attracted to the Cyprus plan. Herzl's recollection was that the foreign secretary's office was like a junk shop whose manager was not quite sure whether some unusual article was in the stockroom. "He's going to take a look and see if England happens to have anything in stock for the Jewish people," Herzl thought to himself. Chamberlain rummaged through a stack of papers and picked out a map, the predominant color of which was red, indicating British imperial acquisitions. After a moment's thought he addressed Herzl: "I say, my good fellow, how about Uganda?"

Herzl was by now desperate for any territory and he accepted the idea as a temporary location. The Sixth Zionist Congress of 1903 rejected the scheme out of hand.

Herzl's diplomatic efforts ended in failure. The next year he was dead. His last testament was a fictional account of the future Jewish State which he titled *Altneuland* (Oldnewland). The book described Herzl's vision of a New Society in which Christian, Muslim and Jew would live in personal freedom and tolerance. In one of its passages, a European asks an Arab inhabitant of the new Jewish State why he doesn't consider the Jew an intruder. The Arab replies: "Would you regard those as intruders and robbers who don't take anything from you but give you something? The Jews have enriched us, why should we be angry at them? They live with us like brothers, why should we not love them?"

Time was to prove that reality wore a different mask from Herzl's vision of the future. Many years later, when Britain was committed to the establishment of the Jewish National Home in Palestine, a European reporter asked the Arab mayor of Nablus what he imagined to be the aims of the Zionist movement. "To take Palestine," the mayor answered simply. Part of the tragedy of modern Palestine was that the Arabs grasped the full implication of the Zionist movement even before many Zionists admitted it frankly to themselves.

Where Herzl had failed, another man was to succeed. Chaim Weizmann came to England from Russia in 1904 at the age of thirty convinced that there lay the strongest potential sympathy for the Zionist cause.[17] Weizmann's sole companion during his first days in London was the kindly Jewish tailor with whom he lodged in Sidney Street. He felt alone and insignificant amid the crowds of London's streets and soon took himself to the quieter life of Manchester where he shed the cloak of solitude. Through local Zionist circles and a post as chemist at the university, he made his first real acquaintance with English life. Ultimately he enjoyed an intimacy with many of England's leading figures in politics and journalism. Among them was C.P. Scott, editor of the influential *Manchester Guardian,* who introduced him to David Lloyd George, a member of the cabinet and future prime minister of Great Britain. By 1907 Weizmann was the leading figure in the Zionist movement, devoted to fulfilling Herzl's political work and to encouraging the actual physical occupation of the land of Palestine by Jewish settlers.

Shortly, two other important Zionists, Sokolov and Tshlenov, joined him from the Continent. Their task was to convert British Jewry to Zionism and to cultivate friendship for the Zionist cause among the highest ranks of His Majesty's Government. The Zionist leaders had easy access to the corridors of power in Whitehall and met often with ministers of the Crown and ranking civil servants in the intimacy of their carpeted, book-lined bureaux. In the end their labors were rewarded, although Gentile enthusiasts were to support their program for a variety of motives, some humorously engaging, others devilish in their effect.

Some saw the restoration of the Jew to Palestine as the fulfillment of biblical prophecy; others were moved by a sense of guilt stemming from a subconscious anti-Semitism. Still other Gentile Zionists confused Zionism with liberalism; the Jewish problem demanded a solution and the most just approach may have appeared to be the national or racial one advocated by the Zionists as against the more genuinely liberal view of the assimilationists. In later years there were more sophisticated arguments suggesting that a Zionist presence in the Middle East was "good" for civilization (European), that the Jews would introduce democracy, modern technology to that unstable part of the world, and generally protect European interests, the Suez Canal in particular. After the Six Day War, Israeli, European and American interests became so closely allied that in France the still anti-Semitic fascists could shout *"Vive l'Israël, à bas les Juifs,"* while right-wing American newspapers carried a host of letters on the theme of defending Israel as the "bastion of Americanism and democracy in the Middle East, the only ally we can rely on."

Zionism made little actual headway until the outbreak of World War I in 1914, when Turkey joined the German side against the Allies. British Prime Minister Asquith remarked that the Ottoman Empire had committed suicide and consequently the policy toward Ottoman Turkey and her Arab provinces had to be reevaluated.

Hostile Ottoman forces in Palestine rendered vulnerable the British occupation of Egypt and the security of the Suez Canal. A Turkish attack on the canal in the early months of the war (February 1915) while unsuccessful, confirmed this view. Moreover, Britain was in stiff economic competition with France for a dominant position in Syria. On the eve of war, Britain and France had concluded separate agreements with Germany which effectively partitioned the Ottoman Arab provinces into economic spheres of influence. Britain's aims were twofold: *first*, to prevent the expansion of any rival European influence into the Persian Gulf and Lower Iraq, and *second*, to secure an outlet on the Mediterranean Sea (preferably at Haifa) as a railhead for a line connecting the gulf with the sea. Therefore, either the control or the neutralization of Palestine with a British naval base close to Egypt would provide a buffer zone to protect the Suez Canal and make Britain the supreme naval force in the entire Mediterranean. French financial, religious and national interests, on the other hand, were striving for exclusive control of the whole of Syria, including Palestine.

World War I was a boon to the Zionist cause, Britain and France needed friends and were ready to bargain in order to get them. It so happened that they bargained with the Zionists and the Arabs at the same time, leading both to believe that the European Allies were on their side.

In the meantime, Weizmann had been considering a line of approach to complement British interests. If Britain were to secure a foothold in Palestine and then encourage Jewish settlement there, the Jews could, he wrote in a letter to C.P. Scott, "develop the country, bring back civilization to it and *form a very effective guard for the Suez Canal.*"[18] Later he thought that if Britain did not want to acquire Palestine as a permanent protectorate the Jews should take over the country under temporary British rule.

By the spring of 1916 the British Government began to give serious consideration to official recognition of the Zionist program. Several factors determined their thinking. These were the difficult months of the war, Britain began to sound out her Allies' reactions to the Zionists' aims bearing in mind that a favorable reception might win over the Jewish populations of Eastern Europe and the United States more positively to the Allied side. Other motives were also apparent. Britain had by then abandoned all pretensions of her "hands off Syria" policy of 1912, and now challenged France's determination to secure undivided control of the area. Military considerations also hastened the need to forestall mutual suspicions between the two allies by formally recognizing each other's spheres of influence.

In October 1915 London informed Paris of her efforts to draw the Arabs to the Allied side against Turkey. France was anxious to have a voice in any agreement which might otherwise be used to the detriment of her own interests in Syria. The two governments decided to settle their claims to the Ottoman Arab provinces by dividing Syria (including Lebanon and Palestine) and Iraq into spheres of influence. The details of the partition were worked out by Sir Mark Sykes, the War Office's leading expert on the Middle East and M. Georges-Picot, who had served as French consul in Beirut before the war.

During the bargaining sessions the British negotiator pressed for the inclusion of Palestine in her sphere. After intensive discussions which nearly exhausted the negotiators, it was finally agreed that the area should be placed under an international regime. Britain received the port of Haifa and a vast zone bordering directly upon the proposed internationalized area, considerably increasing her power in the region of southern Syria. The bulk of the Sykes-Picot agreement, concluded in March 1916, related to railway rights in Syria and Iraq, indicating the concern of the two parties to give diplomatic sanction to their economic and strategic interests.

British Prime Minister Lloyd George was unhappy with the proposed internationalization of Palestine, a view shared by the Zionists. It is quite possible that, as Dr. Frischwasser Ra'anan suggests, "the decision to replace international government by British rule over Palestine was the mainspring behind the policy leading to the Balfour Declaration."[9] As sponsor of the Jewish National Home, Britain would be the logical choice as trustee.

By the fall of 1916 the Zionists were ready to present their program to the British Government. In October they submitted a memorandum to the Foreign Office in which specific mention of a future Jewish state was not included, but where the suggested provisions for the existing Jewish community in Palestine and for the Jewish community-to-be would give the Jews a preferential position in the form of a quasi-government under the suzerainty of either Britain or France. A charter company (originally Herzl's idea) would be incorporated possessing vast powers such as the control of immigration, the right of preemption of Crown lands and the acquisition of all or any concessions which the suzerain government might grant them.

Zionists justified these preferential powers on two grounds: *first*, that the Jewish population of Palestine (which at the time was 10 percent of the total) constituted a distinct national unit, and *second*, that the remaining Arab population "being too small, too poor, and too little trained to make rapid progress, requires the introduction of a new and progressive element in the population, desirous of devoting all its energies and capital to the work of colonization on modern lines."[10]

In the Zionist field of vision the Arab never appeared in sharp focus as a human being of flesh and blood, but rather as a blurred and shadowy figure, indistinct and unreal, a political factor of negligible importance. Herzl would have had the Arab population "*spirited* across the frontier." The verb itself is suggestive. They were also regarded as too small (although 90 percent of the total population), too poor and backward to merit attention. The Zionist motto at the time crystallized the attitude: "Give us, a people without a land, a land without people." The Arab peasant in his field or on the hillside and the artisan in his shop simply did not exist.

The claim of privileged rights for the present and future Jewish inhabitants of Palestine was quite natural. If Palestine were decreed empty of inhabitants, then such rights which Jews would enjoy would not be beyond the common advantage of others, there being no others in this case. But if the embarrassing subject of the Arab population were raised, then the privileges could be shown to benefit the entire population, Arab and Jew, by "the introduction of a new and progressive element" into the country.

Such crusading sentiment was common to nineteenth century colonialist propaganda. The French had argued that their occupation of Algeria would open the continent to "culture and civilization" and the Englishman in Egypt was convinced that his mission was to save Egyptian society. In neither case was the Algerian or Egyptian persuaded that these European civilizing missions were worth the price of domination and occupation.

In any event, the narrow nationalistic Zionist viewpoint demanded the application of a double standard of judgment, one for themselves and the other for the Arabs. For example, in the light of the final formula of the Balfour Declaration, it is interesting to note the distinction which the Zionists drew between Jewish and Arab rights in Palestine. According to their memorandum all inhabitants "regardless of denomination, religion or nationality" should be guaranteed equality of "civic rights" while the Jewish population should enjoy "civic, *political,* and community rights." No Zionist proposal ever mentioned political rights pertaining to the Arabs. The same omission was made in the Balfour Declaration. Zionists protested that such rights for the Arabs were taken for granted. If so, why not take them for granted in their own case? But a more fundamental question is: should political rights ever be taken for granted?

The attitudes of prominent Zionists merely underlined the point. In one of the frequent informal meetings between British

officials and Zionists, Sir Mark Sykes interviewed the Jewish
leaders on the details of their program. He raised the possibility
of an Arab challenge to the Zionist claims. Weizmann retorted
that "the Jews are returning to Palestine for the purpose of
re-creating the Jewish nation and of remaining Jews in the
complete sense, and not to be turned into Arabs, Druze or even
Englishmen."[11] Weizmann's remark was clarified by the
observation he made at about the same time to the effect that
the Zionist movement was similar to the French colonial
enterprise in Tunisia. "What the French could do in Tunisia,"
he said, "the Jews would do in Palestine with Jewish will, Jewish
money, Jewish power and Jewish enthusiasm."[12]

The French colonial regimes in North Africa (and the attitudes
of the French *colons*) were, however, not noted for generous
consideration of the local Arab population.

At that same informal gathering of British civil servants and
Zionists, Sykes suggested that Sokolov meet with M. Georges-
Picot, the French diplomat, to secure his country's support for
their program. Georges-Picot also raised the question of Jewish
relations with the Arabs, and Sokolov replied that "no serious
opposition would be encountered from the Arabs because they
had never regarded Palestine as an important center, particularly
in light of the fact that an Arab dominion was to be set up
elsewhere."[13]

On the assumption that Arabs considered Palestine relatively
unimportant, the winds of change were blowing favorably for
the Zionists and all seemed well, save for one element of
opposition which, if not unexpected, was at least untimely. It
was becoming evident in anti-Zionist Jewish circles that the
British Government was about ready to declare some sort of
open support for the Zionists. This provoked a protest from D.L.
Alexander and Claude Montefiore, respectively president of
the Board of Deputies of British Jews and president of the Anglo-
Jewish Association. In the name of their Conjoint Committee a
manifesto of protest appeared in the London *Times,* May 24,
1917. They attacked the political theories of Zionism as a
threat to the religious basis of Judaism because a secular
Jewish nationality based on some obscure principle of race or
ethnic peculiarity "would not be Jewish in any spiritual sense."

Moreover, the Zionist demands for certain special rights in Palestine which the Arabs would not enjoy was contrary to the principle of equal rights for all religious denominations which Jews in Europe and North America claimed as vital for themselves. If Zionists were to disregard this principle in Palestine, Jews the world over would be convicted of having appealed to it "for purely selfish motives."

The letter ended with the prophetic words that the Zionist scheme was the more inadmissible because it would involve them "in the bitterest feuds with their neighbors of other races and religions," and would "find deplorable echoes throughout the Orient." As a foretaste of the conflict ahead in Palestine, these words had a strange harmony with later Arab warnings. Similar protests were heard from anti-Zionist Jews and non-Jews alike in France and Italy; but their governments too were now virtually committed to the Zionist cause.

The Zionists next got down to the business of drafting their own formula for the declaration. Every word was carefully scrutinized and each phrase weighed for the correct shade of meaning. Possibly no document in diplomatic history has been subjected to such minute attention. After three separate efforts one formula was chosen which covered the essential ground and dealt with the main proposals presented in their memorandum.

The formula was presented to His Majesty's Government on July 8, 1917. It called upon the government to recognize the whole of Palestine as the national home of the Jewish people; the area east of the Jordan River, Transjordan as it was known, was implied in the request. With regard to the Zionists' privileged position in Palestine, the government was to grant "internal autonomy to the Jewish nationality in Palestine, freedom of immigration for Jews, and the establishment of a Jewish National Colonizing Corporation for the resettlement and economic development of the country." While the term "national home" was used instead of "state," the two had become virtually interchangeable. Jewish sovereignty over Palestine was the Zionists' ultimate goal, as Weizmann spelled out to a special congress of the English Federation of Zionists in May of the same year.

Within the cabinet the Zionists could count on the firm

support of Prime Minister Lloyd George, Foreign Secretary
Lord Balfour, and Lords Milner and Cecil. The most incisive
criticism came from the only Jew in the cabinet, Sir Edwin
Montagu, who was the secretary of state for India. Sir Edwin
was the son of Samuel Montagu, a devout and active Orthodox
Jew and the founder of one of London's most important private
banks. The younger Montagu's only nationalism was English,
and he felt that loyalty to another nationalist cause was
tantamount to treason to his native land. His opposition ran
along the lines of the Conjoint Committee's protest. If a Jewish
national home were created, he asked, how could he negotiate
with "the peoples of India on behalf of His Majesty's Government
if the world had just been told that His Majesty's Government
regarded his national home as being in Turkish territory?" Zionists
held him largely responsible for the failure of their draft being
accepted substantially as it was. Weizmann, in fact, expressed
his bewilderment at the attention the British Government gave
to a "handful of assimilated Jews."

The Zionist draft was consequently modified by a cabinet
committee. Like the original, the amended draft made no mention
of the Arab population, but the crucial phrase "National Home"
was retained. In the final version the Arabs were alluded to as
"the existing non-Jewish communities," and the only safeguards
they were given pertained to their civil and religious rights.
A leading Zionist, Jacob de Haas, who had a hand in drafting
the declaration, later admitted that the phrase "political rights"
was deliberately omitted to distinguish Jewish "rights" from
Arab "claims." Since the Arabs had not been consulted on the
matter, they were in effect being told what "claims" they were
entitled to and, by omission, what "rights" they would not
receive.[14]

The final version was dispatched by the cabinet to Washington
to be worked over by Zionists there, and then submitted to
President Wilson for his approval. Only slightly revised, the
formula was returned to London and was issued by the war
cabinet. It was contained in a letter from Lord Balfour to Lord
Walter Rothschild on November 2, 1917:

His Majesty's Government view with favor the establishment

in Palestine of a national home for the Jewish people, and will use their best endeavors to facilitate the achievement of this object, it being clearly understood that nothing shall be done which may prejudice the civil and religious rights of the existing non-Jewish communities in Palestine, or the rights and political status enjoyed by Jews in any other country.

The Balfour Declaration, as it became known, was the product of many hands, minds and months of labor. Despite Zionist participation in its composition, some were less than satisfied. Weizmann records that he was disappointed in the final emasculated version. The original Zionist formula had said that *all* of Palestine should be made the Jewish National Home. In Balfour's version the phrase read "the establishment *in* Palestine" of the national home, meaning *in part* of Palestine. Weizmann's second objection was that the final version "introduced the subject of 'the civil religious rights of the existing non-Jewish communities' in such a fashion as to impute possible oppressive intentions to the Jews, and can be interpreted to mean such limitations on our work as completely to cripple it."[15] The point was, of course, that it should have been unnecessary even to mention the rights of the indigenous population. Preoccupied as they were with obtaining sufficient conditions for the national home, Zionists like Weizmann never seriously considered whether the problem they were attempting to solve would necessarily raise other problems — such as how to deal with the inhabitants of Palestine — which demanded immediate, if only tentative, solutions.

There was instead an awareness of realities, the implications of the declaration being understood by its authors which made a verbal sleight-of-hand politically expedient. Arthur Balfour clearly wanted to see a Jewish state established.

Balfour, the earnest politician, had first been introduced to Zionism during the 1906 general election when he stood as the Conservative candidate in the Clayton division of North Manchester. Charles Dreyfus, a leading industrialist and chairman of both the Manchester Conservative Committee and the local Zionist Society, introduced Chaim Weizmann to Balfour in the course of the campaign. Balfour listened with patient interest to Weizmann's argument, delivered in a difficult and heavy accent. Nevertheless his eloquent and impassioned narrative of the historic longing of the Jews to rebuild their life in Palestine touched the philosopher in Balfour. The two men did not meet again until the beginning of the war, when Balfour, then First Lord of the Admiralty, greeted Weizmann warmly, saying: "You know, I believe that when the guns stop firing you may get your Jerusalem."

However, Balfour, the pragmatic statesman, was aware that the Zionist goal might be made more difficult if precise terminology was employed or if the eventuality of a Jewish state was prematurely discussed in public.[16] Hence the retention of the vague term "Jewish national home" in the declaration. If the Jewish State were the ultimate intention, what then of the promised safeguards of Arab rights? Again, Arthur Balfour was not unmindful of the possible repercussions of a premeditated policy of support for Zionist pretentions in Palestine. In a memorandum written in August 1919, Balfour stated that the Arabs of Palestine would not be consulted concerning their future. "The four Great Powers," he wrote, "are committed to Zionism, and Zionism, be it right or wrong, good or bad, is rooted in age-long tradition, in present needs and future hopes of far profounder import than the desires and prejudices of the 700,000 Arabs who now inhabit that ancient land."[17]

2

"... a Land Without People"

Palestine in history was the fertile bridge between Asia and Africa, the crossroads of three continents and the land of three faiths. The natural endowments of the land, its geographical position and its religious associations attracted many peoples and invaders from the ancient Hebrews, through the Greeks and Romans, the Byzantines, Persians and finally the Arabs.

From the middle of the seventh century Palestine belonged to the Islamic world, at first by the simple act of conquest, and then by degrees, as Islam, the vital cultural force and Arabic, the language of Islamic religious and secular literature, were woven into the fabric of the everyday life of the people.

In the brief space of four years the Muslim armies swept out of their desert fortress in Arabia and overran Iraq, Syria and Palestine. The imperial armies of Byzantium in the west and of Persia in the east, weakened by their own bloody struggle for supremacy in the area, crumbled before the onslaught. Palestine fell before a two-pronged thrust. Amr ibn al-As, one of the most valiant warriors and eminent political figures of early Islam, attacked Palestine from the south via Aqaba and Gaza. Pressing northward after two swift victories against Byzantine forces, he suddenly encountered stiff resistance from the enemy. Amr was in desperate straits until assistance miraculously appeared from an unexpected quarter. The most formidable Arab general of the day, Khalid ibn al-Walid, had been chasing Persians up the Euphrates valley and out of Iraq when he heard of Amr's plight. He force-marched his troops across one thousand trackless, blistering miles of the Syrian desert, joined up with Amr near Jerusalem and routed a vastly superior Byzantine Army. A new chapter in Palestine's long history was about to begin.

Islam and the empire spread rapidly westward across north Africa from Egypt to Morocco, into Spain and eastward beyond Persia into the depths of Central Asia. In this mighty arch of empire, Palestine seemed an insignificant keystone, although it formed the important land bridge between the eastern and western halves.

In a richer, and deeper sense too, this ancient land became part of the Islamic world. After Mecca, the birthplace of the Prophet Muhammad, and Medina his second home, Jerusalem is regarded as the third holiest city in Islam. It is said that one night the angel Gabriel appeared before Muhammad with a white mare and ordered him to mount and follow. The Prophet's nocturnal ride took him to Jerusalem where, on the site of the rock believed to be part of the ruins of Solomon's Temple, he was raised into heaven. In 691 A.D. the Caliph Abd al-Malik erected a cupola over this spot. Known as the Dome of the Rock, this building remains today the finest piece of architecture in the Old City. The sanctity of Jerusalem is well expressed in the tradition related by Ka'b ibn Ahbar, an early Jewish convert to Islam, that each night 70,000 angels descend from heaven to intercede for the pardon of those who have come to the Holy City to pray. It was this same Ka'b who suggested that a mosque be built on the site of the ancient Temple of Solomon.

The Christian and Jewish populations lived in peace with their Muslim rulers. As possessors of their own divinely revealed scriptures, they were respected as People of the Book. They enjoyed certain privileges as protected minorities, although they were also obliged to pay special taxes. Many converted to Islam and over the centuries slowly became Arabized. Palestine enjoyed its claim to be the land of three faiths. Ironically, the two bitterest periods of enmity which Palestine has witnessed came about as the result of European intrusion. The first was during the Crusades when Jews were massacred in Jerusalem and Tiberias by the invading Christian armies. Jews and Muslims were brothers-in-exile until the Crusaders were finally driven from the Middle East. The second occasion came after World War I when Christian and Muslim Arabs of Palestine allied in their struggle against the British Mandate and its policy of a Jewish National Home. Today the Arab struggle against Israel is seen by the Arabs as a fight to liberate a part of their homeland from foreign occupation.

At the dawning of the nineteenth century Palestine was, as it had been for centuries, Arab in character, an integral part socially, economically and politically of the Fertile Crescent which included Syria, Lebanon and Iraq. At that time the Fertile Crescent as a whole comprised several provinces of the Ottoman Empire. The administrative divisions of Palestine, for example, reflected the political integration. West of the Jordan River, the northern half of Palestine was part of the Vilayet of Beirut; the southern half was known as the Sanjak of Jerusalem and was governed directly from Constantinople (the Istanbul of modern Turkey). The area east of the Jordan was part of the Vilayet of Damascus. Palestine, in fact, was regarded by the Arabs as southern Syria.

The country's main source of wealth was the fertile land which supported a peasantry engaged in the traditional methods of cultivation. A fertile coastal plain, varying in width, stretched from Gaza in the south to Acre in the north. There the belt of green described a gentle curve from the Plain of Acre to the Plain of Esdraelon resting between the Carmel range of mountains and the Galilean hills to the Vale of Jezreel which approached the Jordan River south of Lake Tiberias.

There are no glossy colored photographs of Palestine dating from the early nineteenth century. Fortunately, however, the English produced men and women who were not content with the beauties of their own sceptered isle. Lady Hester Stanhope, a remarkable Englishwoman who gratified a lust for adventure with a life of travel, visited Palestine in 1810. In her diary she recorded the variety of plain and mountain, hill and valley, river and lake which the country presented to her admiring eye. "The luxuriance of vegetation is not to be described," she wrote. "Fruits of all sorts from the banana down to the blackberry are abundant. The banks of the rivers are clothed naturally with oleander and flowering shrubs."

Laurence Oliphant wrote in 1883 that the Plain of Esdraelon, where a Beirut family had large holdings, "is at this moment in a high state of cultivation. It looks today like a huge green lake of waving wheat, with its village-crowned mounds rising from it like islands and it presents one of the most striking pictures of luxurious fertility which it is possible to conceive." The terraced cultivation of Judea moved John Brinton to exclaim in 1891: "Here is one more among the thousand proofs of the ancient prosperity of the land." The words of an anonymous scribe are preserved in the Bible: Palestine in ancient times was a land "flowing with milk and honey," a phrase which has become symbolic for abundance and plenty. In more precise language Lady Stanhope described the Arab orchards near Jaffa as containing "lemon, orange, almond, peach, apple, pomegranate and other trees." These were the milk and honey of the inhabitants.

But Palestine presented another aspect. The Jordan River might be bordered with oleander and flowering shrubs, but the hills which rose on either side of the valley were stark, barren and inhospitable to man or beast. South of the Judean Plateau the Negev Desert ran as far as the eye could see and lost itself in the empty wastes of Sinai. Apart from a small nomadic population, the desert supported no permanent settlements. Only in recent times have modern men and machines dared to tame this natural wilderness.

The peasant worked the land by traditional means, the hand hoe and bullock-drawn plow, and in normal times his labors yielded a harvest of plenty. Some years there was want, for a plague of locusts could bring destruction to a field of wheat more swifty than invasion by enemy infantry. Through times of plenty and want the peasant lived by the simple ethic that he would take from the soil what God had given him, and give to others from what he had. By 1900 the picture had changed very little, although a few citrus growers had begun to import motorized pumps to irrigate their orchards. The products of the land, the citrus fruits and the cereal grains were shipped to all parts of Syria. The famous olive oil soap of Nablus and Jaffa, which was used for ritual purposes, also reached wide markets in the Muslim Near East. Other home industries operated, but on a much smaller scale. Clothing, carpets and rugs were made by workers in their homes or in small workshops in the towns. Silk worms were cultivated at Acre. Objects of piety carved from olive wood or made from imported mother-of-pearl were to be found in the artisan shops of Jerusalem. Wine was produced in Christian monasteries and in Jewish settlements established by Baron Edmund Rothschild at the end of the last century. For the modest needs of the times, Palestine was remarkably self-sufficient. (did it really need European influence?)

Although the country was overwhelmingly rural in character, the urban population comprised members of the landowning class, the religious hierarchies, professional people, artisans, trade merchants and shopkeepers. The educated were few. Christians enjoyed the facilities of European mission schools, but for their higher education they would travel to Beirut to attend either the American Protestant College or the French Collège Saint-Joseph. Muslims pursued higher learning mainly in the traditional Islamic sciences of theology, philosophy, language and literature at either the metropolis of Constantinople or at the famous 900-year-old University of al-Azhar in Cairo. The vast majority of the population was Muslim, while important concentrations of Arab Christians lived in Jerusalem, Nazareth and Bethlehem. Arab Jews resided in Jerusalem, Safad and Tiberias.

At the outbreak of World War I Palestinians were neither a separate people nor a nation. As Arabs and subjects of the Ottoman sultan they did exist *in* Palestine, the land which was their home and where their forefathers had for centuries past lived and left their graves.

Palestine was neither desolate nor uninhabited.

Even Balfour was to admit that Palestinians had their "desires and prejudices," many of which they shared with their fellow Arabs in Syria, Lebanon, Iraq and Egypt. The Arabs' view of the world and the part they sought to play in it were products of a historical situation molded in the previous century both by forces within the Arab community and by the broader cultural encounter with the West. These factors conditioned the Arabs' reaction to post-war developments and to Zionist aims.

By the middle of the eighteenth century the Ottoman Empire, which included the Arab provinces in Egypt and the Fertile Crescent, had begun its decline. The weakening of the military, economic and moral fibers of the empire was occasioned by the rapid technological advances being made in various European countries which were then able to increase their diplomatic and commercial influence at Constantinople. At the same time, the weakening of the central authority meant that Constantinople could no longer command the undivided loyalty of its citizens, nor act as the main focus of solidarity.

Local forces in the Fertile Crescent began to assert their autonomy, although nominally acting in the sultan's interests. Moreover, Ottoman Christians began to cultivate an interest in their own Christian and Arab heritage. While these movements struck at the traditional principles of solidarity of the empire, the Arab provinces themselves remained completely isolated from the ferment of new ideas. They were oblivious to any threat of rising European power and secure in a complacent belief in the superiority of their own inner, yet static, resources.

This atmosphere of blissful complacency was rudely shattered by the sudden and unexpected invasion of Egypt by Napoleon in 1798, and his abortive attack on Palestine in the following year. By this act Napoleon unleashed a tidal wave of new ideas — military, political and socio-economic — on traditional Mediterranean life. He gave birth to what one writer has called the "Arab rediscovery of Europe." From the time of the French invasion to the decade of the eighteen-seventies the Arab world was uprooted from its isolation, and embroiled in European cultural and political rivalries.

In Egypt Muhammad Ali made the initial response to the European presence, aiming to build a viable state patterned along current western models. Small missions of students were sent to Europe to study the new techniques. Schools of engineering, medicine, pharmaceutics, minerology and agriculture were founded. A school of translation was entrusted with the task of providing Arabic versions of (largely) French and Italian "textbooks." Western ideas filtered into Arab society through channels opened by Muhammad Ali. An Arab image of the Western world began to take concrete form.

Of no less importance in this process of acculturation was the effect of the narratives of Arab travelers to Europe who described and attempted to interpret western society for Arab readers. These impressions of European social and political institutions gradually became a part of the mainstream of Arab cultural awareness. The principle of constitutionalism, or the rule of law as against the rule of the autocrat, captured their attention as it embodied the concepts of justice, equality and freedom. Admiration was also expressed for various welfare, economic and cultural institutions such as hospitals, corporations, libraries and museums, associations which were organized on the initiative of private individuals or groups.

The organizational basis of European society was emphasized in all of the travelers' accounts, and to it they attributed the success of European society. It was believed that Arabs could achieve similar success by adopting western patterns of organization and the superiority of European technology and organization was openly acknowledged. On the other hand, some of them expressed a natural defensiveness because they did not concede the *inherent* superiority of all facets of western culture. Rather, they urged the adoption of what was genuinely strong in order to recapture the earlier moment of the Islamic world's greatness.

By 1870 a generally favorable and comprehensive image of the Western world had been transmitted to the Arab world, for the most part by devout Muslims such as Rifa'a Tahtawi of Egypt and Khayr ad-Din of Tunisia. Christians too, particularly in the Fertile Crescent, were contributing significantly to the Arab awakening. That area of Turkish rule had been opened up to western missionaries and commercial enterprises during the decade of the eighteen-thirties under the enlightened rule of Muhammad Ali's son Ibrahim Pasha.

French and American mission schools were established alongside government-financed institutions. The new wave of learning produced some men of outstanding literary talent who dedicated themselves to the revival of the humanistic spirit in Arabic literature and language. Butrus Bustani compiled a two-volume Arabic dictionary and completed six volumes of an encyclopedia which was continued by other members of his family after his death. Mar'un an-Naqqash, who was influenced by the Italian theater, wrote and produced the first Arabic play and thus introduced a new art form into Arabic literature. The first political novel in Arabic was written by Francis Marrash on the themes of liberty, equality and social justice.

Finally, the historical novels of Jurji Zaydan recalled the
romance of the Arab past in the manner of Sir Walter Scott in
his Waverley novels. Muslims were late in joining this new
movement of self-expression and it was not until 1857 that
Muslims first associated with Christians in the Syrian Scientific
Society which was founded in that year.

The climate of revival and awakening in the Arab world was
accompanied by an intensified European interest in its political
developments. Britain, for example, played a leading role in
driving Ibrahim Pasha from Syria in 1840. Fourteen years later
the Crimean War was fought partly to decide the conflicting
interests of Britain, France and Russia in the area. Again in
1860, civil disturbances in Lebanon brought about European
intervention and the occupation of the country by French troops.
The opening of the Suez Canal in 1869 suddenly provided easy
access to European imperial domains in the Far East and
served to embroil the entire Mediterranean seaboard in the
arena of European politico-economic rivalry. Indeed, Britain
finally occupied Egypt in 1882, ostensibly to safeguard her own
and French financial interests. In 1899 the Sudan was also
occupied by Britain. The French seized what they could of the
North African coast – Tunisia in 1881, Libya and Morocco in
1912.

Events after 1870 seemed to accelerate. The spirit of Arab
renaissance, Arab awareness of a New World and the tightening
grip of western influence combined to complicate the problems
of Ottoman Sultan Abdul Hamid. The empire was threatened,
at least potentially, from within should the Arab revival assume
a more political and anti-Turkish direction. From without, the
empire was definitely threatened by ever increasing European
pressures.

The sultan's Arab subjects were confronted with their own
dilemma. Between 1870 and the outbreak of war in 1914, Syria
was pregnant with various shades of nationalist sentiment.
Christians tended to identify with the idea of an independent
and greater Syria in which all citizens of the Arab nation shared
a common cultural bond irrespective of inherited religious
beliefs. Muslims were equally conscious of their Arab heritage,
but they were hesitant to sever their religious ties with the

sultan and the empire. The Young Turk revolution against Abdul Hamid in 1908 raised their hopes that equal rights for all Arabs, whether Christian or Muslim, could be secured within a decentralized empire. But when the Young Turks themselves retreated into a narrow racist pan-Turkism they unwittingly reinforced the Arabs' consciousness of their own identity.

Secret political societies were formed in which Palestinians played a role. For these activities some of them were later executed by the Turks. The aim of these groups was complete independence. Their call went out to all Arabs — Muslim, Christian and Jew — to unite and break away from Ottoman control. Still the tension of loyalties remained. Would the focus of solidarity be the Turkish Empire or the Arab Nation, Islam or Arabism? The final and decisive step was not taken until 1918 when, as British Prime Minister Asquith had foreseen at the beginning of the war, the Ottoman Empire committed suicide. There was, by then, no alternative to nationalism. With the empire gone the problem of Turkey was replaced by the problem of European imperialism.

The "Arab rediscovery of Europe" opened new vistas to Arab imagination, new visions for the future. Arab society, adopting the organizational patterns of the European nations, could achieve similar successes. This was the vision. But the contact with Europe had brought another and altogether undesirable circumstance: domination and occupation. All of North Africa had fallen under European control, and France and Britain were keenly competing for the rest of the Arab world, particularly the Fertile Crescent.

The wartime generation of Arabs was alive to the dangers of further European encroachment. They had been deeply influenced by the ideas and career of the revolutionary activist and religious thinker, Jamal ad-Din al-Afghani (1838-1897).

Al-Afghani had a passionate spirit and was a fiery orator. His energies were phenomenal. He had been involved in the politics of Afghanistan, studied among Indian Muslims and was the founder and leader of a secret society of young Egyptians who were discontented with the growing European influence over their country. When he was expelled for these activities, he moved to Paris where he edited a newspaper calling for

resistance to the European presence in the Middle East. From
Paris he traveled to Russia and England, ending his days in
Constantinople as a forced "guest" of the sultan. Al-Afghani's
theme was the same wherever he went: Muslim peoples had
allowed themselves to be ruled by reactionary autocrats whose
misgovernment made them prey to the unbridled ambitions of
the European powers. He attributed the deplorable weakness of
the Muslim world to the loss of religious solidarity which had
once led them to embrace half the world. But solidarity could
also be embedded in the national language, the means of
transmitting the Arab national heritage. Religious solidarity was,
in fact, national solidarity and vice versa. Al-Afghani's appeal
went out to all, from the intellectual to the humblest peasant.
To the latter he cried: "Wretched peasant, you break the heart
of the earth to feed yourself and your family. Why do you not
break the heart of your oppressor who eats the fruit of your
labor?"

    Al-Afghani had struck the one chord in harmony with the
deepest aspiration of all Arabs: to recapture and reconstruct
their national independence — their freedom from Turkish
and European control. For many Arabs the war opened the door
of promise and fulfillment. The result was an unlocked Pandora's
box.

which one?

3

A Game of Nations

At one point in her journey through Wonderland, Alice joins the Hatter, the March Hare and the Doormouse for tea. It was a Mad Tea Party. Alice was offended by the scatter-brained behavior of her hosts. Conversation always seemed to run in circles. "Why don't you say what you mean?" the March Hare asked.

"I do," Alice hastily replied. "At least — at least I mean what I say — that's the same thing you know."

"Not the same a bit!" said the Hatter. "Why you might just as well say that 'I see what I eat' is the same thing as 'I eat what I see'."

In the innocent world of fantasy the consequences of a character's actions are only as serious as the author's imagination permits. In the arena of international politics the failure to say what you mean might be construed as deceit; the failure to mean what you say might be interpreted as hypocrisy. The repercussions of either could be momentous. For Palestine they were tragic.

During the First World War, Britain and the Arabs reached an understanding on their respective wartime aims. The understanding was contained in an exchange of diplomatic notes between Sir Henry McMahon, the British high commissioner in Egypt, and Sherif Hussein ibn Ali, the paramount leader in the Arabian peninsula who controlled the Hijaz and the holy places of Mecca and Medina. McMahon expressed his government's sympathy with "the aspirations of her friends the Arabs," and its desire to see "the liberation of the Arab peoples from the Turkish yoke." Hussein stressed the determination of the Arab nation "to assert its right to live, gain its freedom and administer its own affairs in name and in fact."

As a result of reports reaching London of anti-Turkish unrest
in Syria, the British Government was anxious to draw the support
of "the Arab nation" to the Allied side. Once Turkey had
joined the Germans, Arab support became imperative, even if
only passively given. The ideals of Arab liberation and independence were therefore necessarily linked in the British view
with the practical objective of destroying Turkey. After some
hesitation Sherif Hussein raised a revolt against the Turk in
the Arabian peninsula. Regardless of the value attached to Arab
cooperation with the Allies during the war, when that conflict
ended the belief was widespread among all Arabs that they
were about to realize their dream of liberation.

It was during this period that a slightly built, blue-eyed
Englishman stepped into the pages of history immortalized by
his own brilliant prose and the eulogies of his biographers. The
man was Thomas Edward Lawrence, the "Lawrence of Arabia"
of fact and fancy. A complex creature, Lawrence was a competent
linguist and scholar, an expert on crusader fortifications, an
errant soldier and adventurer, and an arrogant romantic.
Lawrence is best remembered for what he wished to be
remembered: his daring exploits during the Arab revolt of
1916, the story of which he recounts with passionate vividness in
his *Seven Pillars of Wisdom.* During the post-war peace negotiations
in London and Paris, he was the constant companion of his
comrade-in-arms Prince Faysal, King Hussein's son. Faysal's
sole contact with the bewildering world of international
political maneuvering was through Lawrence, his interpreter.
Although he was mentor and confidant to a man who had
come to seek independence for his people, Lawrence was not
the anti-colonialist which his more fervent admirers, like Lowell
Thomas, have wished to make of him. He believed deeply in the
greatness of England and empire and held what were, at best,
uncharitable opinions of "native" peoples. He was also the
francophobe who had once declared that if the Arab revolt
were successful, England could "biff the French out of all hope
in Syria." Lawrence died only to triumph over obscurity through
the labors of his publicists. His effect on the course of actual
events in the Middle East was negligible.

By 1918 the relationship between the Arabs and the Allies

had changed. Britain and France concluded their secret pact, the Sykes-Picot agreement of 1916, which, by dividing the Fertile Crescent into spheres of European influence, set the Allies' aims completely at odds with Arab aspirations. The goals of Britain and France did not stem from sudden inspiration, but from the pre-war rivalry of the two nations in which the Middle East assumed an ever increasing importance. The Arab leaders, although suspicious of Allied intentions, failed to comprehend the competitive and expansionist significance of the interests of France and Britain in their lands. The destruction of Turkey, and with it the Ottoman Empire, suited western imperialist interests better than the Arabs' desires for independence.

The diplomatic partition of the Arab East gave way to a military partition which became effective in the last years of the war. Between December 1916 and December 1917, el-Arish, Rafa, Beersheba and Jerusalem were occupied by British forces under General Allenby. A second British expedition had overrun the Turkish position in Iraq. By October 1918, Damascus had fallen and the rout of the Turk was almost complete. Palestine was placed under British military rule and Lebanon under the French. The interior of Syria remained under Arab control for two more years by which time the French had occupied Damascus by force.

The Allies kept up the façade of sympathy for Arab aspirations. A temporary embarrassment was caused by the Russian Revolution. In 1917 the Bolsheviks disclosed the details of the Sykes-Picot agreement (to which czarist Russia had been a party) from documents unearthed in the Russian Foreign Office. Hussein promptly demanded an explanation from British officials concerning the alleged division of Syria and Iraq. Early in February 1918, he received a note from the acting British agent in Jedda, J.R. Bassett, who stressed his government's pledge "to stand steadfastly by the Arabs," who were struggling for "liberation" and "unity." Reginald Wingate, McMahon's successor in Cairo, assured Hussein that the Sykes-Picot agreement was not a treaty but only "a record of old conversations and provisional understandings." Hussein remained unconvinced by these vague, not to say mendacious, replies.

The British Government further clarified its position in June

1918, in a reply to a petition presented by seven leading Syrians. Britain's declaration made two points.

First, the future regimes in those areas liberated and occupied by the Allied armies would be "based upon the principle of the consent of the governed." At the time of this declaration the liberated and occupied areas included the southern half of Palestine up to a line running from Jaffa to Jerusalem. The principle of consent of the governed was an important advance on previous declarations since it implied some method of canvassing the peoples' opinion on their political future and then basing the form of government on that expressed view.

Second, the declaration stated that His Majesty's Government was committed to securing the freedom and independence of all other territory still under Turkish control.

These pledges and declarations collectively should have put all Arab apprehensions to rest. But disturbing questions continued to torment the minds of Arab leaders. Would the principle of the consent of the governed be applied to areas not yet "liberated," such as the northern half of Palestine and the rest of the Fertile Crescent? Did "freedom" mean only freedom from Turkish rule, or freedom from all foreign rule? Was "independence" consistent with the rumored establishment of European spheres of influence?

Finally, in an effort to dispel the growing atmosphere of suspicion and disquiet, Britain and France issued a joint declaration on November 7, 1918. The principle of the consent of the governed was reiterated, and the declaration went on to say that "far from wishing to impose this or that system upon the population of those regions, their (France's and Britain's) only concern is to offer such support and efficacious help as will ensure the smooth working of the governments and administrations which those populations will have elected of their own free will."

This was the last wartime pledge made by the Allies to the Arabs. From the McMahon-Hussein correspondence to the Anglo-French declaration, words such as freedom, independence, self-determination were used with an apparent air of sincerity. They were ideals which many Arabs had come to believe reflected what was best in European society. The Arab travelers to Europe during the nineteenth century had never wearied of praising European attitudes toward the rule of law embodying concepts of justice, equality and freedom. There was, therefore, a predisposition or attraction to aspects of western culture. At the same time Arabs could not but evince feelings of loyalty to the familiar and tested values of their own culture and express conviction in the validity of their own heritage. This produced an essentially ambivalent attitude toward the West which revealed the Arabs' lack of self-confidence and an awareness of their weakness in the face of the material superiority of European power.

It would have been difficult enough for some measure of understanding and respect to have been created between the Arabs and the West after the war. But Britain and France could not, or at least did not, give of their best to the Arab peoples. Liberalism was decaying in Europe. Although "Christian" nations, both Britain and France were also giants of empire and of modern technological societies. Hard work and technology had made these nations successful and success implied to Europeans a moral superiority, a morality which was protected by a superior religion. Moreover, Zionism and European civilization had a common denominator, the association with the Old Testament out of which evolved the concept of a Judeo-Christian heritage. Jews had also been active participants in creating the superior civilization which the Europeans claimed for themselves.

On all counts the Arabs were, in their eyes, wholly outside the "civilized" world. Moreover, the inherited prejudices against Islam, both as a culture and a religion, seemed to justify the application of a double standard of judgment. Progressive society abhors the vacuum created by static society, and despite the Arabs' acceptance of the principle of progress, their resistance to assimilation would not be tolerated by the dominating European power. The European could admit the legitimacy of the Arabs' struggle for independence and freedom, but would not concede that they should shoulder the responsibility for freedom gained.

The wartime ideals were substituted for the baser currency of the concept of "a sacred trust of civilization," to quote the phrase from the Covenant of the League of Nations. The Paris Peace Conference approved the Covenant (April 1919) which had piously asserted that it was the "sacred trust of civilization" to assume responsibility for the "well-being and development... of peoples not yet able to stand by themselves under the strenuous conditions of the modern world." The instruments of this sacred mission, a euphemism for imperial ambitions, were the mandates established in the name of the League by Britain in Iraq and Palestine and by France in Syria and Lebanon. The Covenant had stated that the Arab provinces of the defunct Ottoman Empire were provisionally recognized as independent, subject only "to the rendering of administrative advice and assistance by a mandatory." The wishes of the Arabs themselves had to be a "principal consideration" in the selection of the mandatory power.

Arab opinion, however, was known to be almost unanimously for absolute independence and against the separation of Palestine from the rest of Syria. This meant an unqualified rejection of the Zionist program which Britain was sponsoring. Nevertheless, without reference to the finer sentiments of the Covenant, the mandates were imposed on the Arab East. At the same time, the least advanced region of the Arab world, the Arabian peninsula, was judged by civilization fit for the rigors of modern life and was not assigned to the supervision of a mandate.

Professor Hourani of Oxford has observed that from the creation of the mandate system in the Middle East "there sprang a new moral relationship between the West and the Arab peoples..." Each of the regimes set up by Britain and France shared certain characteristics: they were imposed and maintained by force against the expressed opposition of politically articulate sections of the Arab population. Moreover, the rights and aspirations of the subject peoples were never the primary concern of the controlling powers, despite eloquent declarations from London and Paris to the contrary. "It is this imposition of an alien rule upon an unwilling people which is called 'imperialism'... the essence of imperialism is to be found in a moral relationship — that of power and powerlessness — and any material consequences which spring from it are not enough to change it."[11]

It was in Palestine that the mandate system inflicted the deepest wounds and left a legacy of enduring bitterness and enmity. Britain had virtually declared Palestine a political *tabula rasa;* the Zionists called Palestine a land without a people, which amounted to the same thing. British military authorities in Jerusalem had been informed confidentially by London that the Anglo-French Declaration, which had been issued in Jerusalem, was not to be applied to Palestine. Lord Balfour had said privately that "in the case of Palestine we deliberately and rightly decline to accept the principle of self-determination." Palestine was to be molded, fashioned, hammered into any shape desired; the Palestinians counted for nothing.

The tactics of legal argumentation, adopted by Palestinian leaders at the time to demonstrate that the wartime pledges included their people as well, served only to underline the actual weakness of their position. Foreign troops occupied the country and the military administration was in effective control. Britain and the Zionists viewed Palestine through the spectacles of the imperialist and the colonialist, and by doing so invited the inevitable consequence — violence. The Arab of Palestine would, sooner or later, be forced to the violent self-assertion that he was *something,* if only to prove it to himself. He would demand recognition that he was not a "non-Jew," but an Arab, and that he had not only "civil and religious" rights but political rights as well.

In a curious way the Palestine Mandate obscured the initial source of conflict. The Royal Commission, reporting on "disturbances" in Palestine in 1936, described the overall conflict as a clash of Arab and Jewish nationalisms and that it was "fundamentally a conflict between right and right." This judgment overlooked (as it is too often overlooked today) the basic relationship of force upon which the system was based. The terms of the Mandate were worked out between the Zionists and the British Government. The Balfour Declaration was mentioned in the preamble of the document, and Britain was to be "responsible for placing the country under such political, administrative and economic conditions as will secure the establishment of the Jewish National Home." In effect the relationship of force between Britain and the Arabs of Palestine was to be transposed through the introduction of alien Zionist rule.

4

"What is Ours, is Ours..."

The pattern of conflict in Palestine rapidly crystallized. By 1918 Arab reaction had mounted against the British and their Zionist protégés. During the two years of military administration tension increased to the point where violent Arab riots erupted in the spring of 1920 against British garrisons and Jewish settlements. A court of enquiry reported that the underlying cause of unrest was "a disappointment at the non-fulfillment" of British wartime promises. This was true as far as it went, but popular unrest among the Palestinians seems to have emerged before the war.

Arabs had first encountered Zionist pioneers in the early eighteen-eighties when small groups of young Russian Jews, inspired by the ideals of Leo Pinsker, emigrated to the Holy Land. These newcomers were ill-prepared and poorly financed for the adventure. Many died of disease, some of discouragement. Progress in their settlements was slow and arduous, but for those that remained and survived it was work well done.

Arab reaction to the newcomers was mixed. In some parts of the country cordial relations between Arab and Jew did exist. Jewish settlers required labor and hired Arabs to work their farms, and so Jewish farmer and Arab laborer came to know each other on intimate terms. Arab landowners also came in contact with the new colonists, the one trading his superior knowledge of the land for the other's superior technical skills. It was sometimes found that Arab and Jew owned flocks of sheep in common. Bad times were met in the same spirit as good times. Boundary disputes arose, but were settled over a cup of bitter coffee. Both Arab and Jew faced the common danger of Bedouin raids on their lands, but this was not a threat to their existence.

In other parts of the country developments occurred which bore the seeds of later enmity. In the decade preceding the outbreak of the war the second great wave of Jewish immigrants, the second *aliya* as it is known, brought about 40,000 Jews to Palestine, mainly from Russia and Poland. Most of these men and women were dedicated, militant Zionist idealists. None more so than one David Green, who was to adopt the Hebrew name of Ben Gurion. He and other members of the second *aliya* became prominent figures in the Zionist political elite during the Mandate. It was this group of immigrants which created the image of the pioneer settler, the *halutz*.

Ben Gurion has left a stirring account of his early days in Galilee.[11] He describes the pioneer experience of building new settlements as being "a partner in the act of creation." Always the tough taskmaster, Ben Gurion was supremely Jewish in everything he did. Some have made the comparison with Cecil Rhodes in South Africa, and from a personal comparison Rhodes must come off second best. A man of few vices, David Ben Gurion set out to impart to an unwilling people a stern morality based on an agricultural vocation which was strange to their European tradition and desires. That in large part he succeeded is a testament to the man's physical and spiritual fortitude.

Writing much like an Old Testament prophet, he admonished his pioneer brothers for diluting their farm force with Arab guards. Everything had to be Jewish if it was to be a real and permanent return to the Promised Land. He spared no one, not even the pioneers of his kibbutz at Sejera, in Galilee: "Even here the purity of our aspirations was clouded. The fields were worked, it is true, by Jewish hands, but their watchmen were hired Arabs... Jewish labor, our labor, was the rule; the place was alive with Jewish youngsters — could we entrust all that to strange hands? Was it conceivable that we should be hiring strangers to guard our property and protect our lives?"

The Arab watchmen were "diligent in their work and outstanding for courage and spirit," Ben Gurion wrote. Even so, and despite their excellent qualities, they were nevertheless the foe, and some of the younger men decided that hostilities had to be directed against their watchmen in order to convince the

farm supervisor that Jews alone should manage their own affairs.
Employing various stratagems, the Zionist pioneers succeeded
in having the Arab guards replaced by their own people. The
campaign was completed, Ben Gurion recalls, only when the
settlement had founded its own permanent militia which, of
course, required a sizeable supply of arms. The arms were
forthcoming and so, in time, was open conflict between the
Jewish settlers and the Arabs.

These developments were not viewed lightly by the Arabs.[2]
The implications of Jewish immigration and land purchases
began to dawn on them, and the Arabic press warned its readers
that a Jewish state was the Zionists' final goal. Anti-Zionist
groups sprang up in Jerusalem, Haifa and Nablus, drawing
support from the younger, more politically conscious elements.
Slowly, popular unrest began to grow. One Arab notable from
Jerusalem, who was not unfriendly to the Zionists, warned them
that although governments may come and go, "the people are
the constant factor; one must come to agreement with the
people." For their part, the Zionists realized that there could
be no measure of compromise on the questions of immigration
and land purchases for on these two pillars their assured
supremacy in Palestine would be built.

Zionists were proud Europeans who shared with their
Christian fellows what was, at best, a paternalistic attitude
toward "native" peoples, at worst open contempt. Perhaps,
unlike classical colonial ventures, they did not seek to dominate
the native population. But the construction of the National
Home made the exclusion of the Arab implicit. Their view of
the Arab contained a kind of self-fulfilling prophecy. They
assumed the Arab was their enemy, implacably determined
to destroy the cherished ideals for which Zionism stood. He
had to be resisted at every turn. When the Arab finally turned
violently against those who sought to exclude him, possibly even
to eliminate him, the original assumption was proven correct
and the prophecy fulfilled.

When Zionists attempted to transform their ideals into
practice, it seemed to the Arab that their actions gave the lie to
the genuineness of those ideals. In his *Road to Jerusalem*,
historian Barnet Litvinoff has neatly summarized this Zionist

attitude. Theirs was "a ruthless doctrine, calling for monastic self-discipline and cold detachment from environment. The Jews who gloried in the name of socialist worker interpreted brother-hood on a strictly nationalist, or racial basis, for they meant brotherhood with Jew, not with Arab. As they insisted on working the soil with their own hands, since exploitation of others was anathema to them, they excluded the Arabs from their regime... They believed in equality, but for themselves. They lived on Jewish bread raised on Jewish soil that was protected by a Jewish rifle."[13]

Other factors contributed to the disturbances of 1920 which were the initial steps taken toward the establishment of the Jewish National Home. The British cabinet had authorized the Zionist Organization to form its own commission ostensibly for the purpose of carrying on relief work in the Jewish community of Palestine which, like the rest of the population, had been badly hit by the war. The commission's definition of status also made it a representative body of the World Zionist Organization in Palestine to act in an advisory capacity to the military administration on all matters which might effect "the establishment of a national home for the Jewish people in accordance with the (Balfour) Declaration." The Zionist Com-mission, therefore, had a definite political function and, consequently, ran into difficulties with the military administration which, under international convention, was obliged to preserve the status quo of the occupied country and keep its institutions intact.

Dr. Weizmann, who was head of the commission, recognized the administration's position and also the need to dispel Arab apprehensions concerning the commission's work. He spoke to a group of Arab notables in Jerusalem, saying that "all fears expressed openly or secretly by the Arabs that they are to be ousted from their present position are due either to a fundamental misconception of Zionist aims or to the malicious activities of our common enemies." The inner meaning of Jewish aspirations, he said, was the longing for a moral and spiritual center to bind Jewish tradition of the past with the future. Weizmann, however, addressed himself to a very different purpose in discussions with representatives of the Palestinian Jewish

Uses political data to explain the development of the Arab Sentiments

community who expected the imminent creation of the Jewish
State. Weizmann argued that since the Jews lacked the power,
the time had not yet come to found the state. Instead "we must
ask for some strong government, which we may trust to administer
our 'state' justly, to take matters under its direction, enable us to
develop our abilities, our institutions and our colonies until
the time comes when we shall be fit to undertake the administration
of the country ourselves."[14] As for the Arabs of Palestine, they
were now convinced that they labored under no "fundamental
misconception" of Zionist aims.

The Zionist Commission made numerous demands of the
military administration in an attempt to alter the status quo.
They were successful in having Hebrew recognized as an
official language and in setting up a land commission to investigate
development prospects of the country. Other demands were rejected
as excessive, such as the transfer to the Zionists of some quarter
of a million acres of land under state domain. These were the
urban and rural properties of German colonists near Jaffa, and
even the French-owned Jaffa-Jerusalem railway. The Zionist
Commission also sought to increase Jewish participation in the
administration (the twenty odd senior executive posts were held
by the British, nine of whom were Jews) at a time when no
Arab participation was permitted.

Great Arab resentment was caused by the Zionist Commission's
opposition to the administration's granting of agricultural loans
to farmers. The assets of the Ottoman Agricultural Bank from
which the farmers used to obtain cheap credit had been carried
away by the Turks when their army was driven from Palestine.
In the difficult economic conditions brought about by the war
it was imperative that the farmers acquire capital advances in
order to rebuild their farms and orchards. The commission
demanded that the power of granting loans be entrusted to the
Anglo-Palestine Bank, a Zionist enterprise. The administration
balked at these demands and the timely intervention of Weizmann
caused the matter to be dropped. Further damage to Arab-
Jewish relations, however, had already been done.

At the time of the 1920 crisis, the chief administrator, Sir
Louis Bols, severely criticized the commission's activities and
attitudes in a report to London:

(The Zionist Commission) seek not justice from the military occupant but that in every question in which a Jew is interested discrimination in his favor shall be shown...

It is unnecessary to press my difficulty... in controlling any situation that may arise in the future if I have to deal with a representative of the Jewish community who threatens me with mob law and refuses to accept the constituted forces of law and order...

It is no use saying to the Moslem and Christian elements of the population that our declaration as to the maintenance of the status quo made on our entry into Jerusalem has been observed. Facts witness otherwise: the introduction of the Hebrew tongue as an official language; the setting up of a Jewish judicature; the whole fabric of government of the Zionist Commission of which they are well aware; the special traveling privileges to members of the Zionist Commission; this has firmly and absolutely convinced the non-Jewish elements of our partiality. On the other hand, the Zionist Commission accuse my officers and me of anti-Zionism. The situation is intolerable...[5]

Sir Louis recommended that in the interests of peace the Zionist Commission be abolished. Instead of acting upon this recommendation, the British cabinet decided instead to abolish the military administration! The first British high commissioner, Sir Herbert Samuel, initiated the civil administration of Palestine in July 1920.

Sir Herbert's unenviable task was to give effect to the Balfour Declaration which was then being written into the terms of the Mandate. He was charged with the duty of creating in Palestine such political and economic conditions as would secure the establishment of the Jewish National Home, while at the same time safeguarding the rights of the majority Arab population.

Although he proved to be an extremely able and fair administrator, Sir Herbert's choice as high commissioner was unfair to both the man and the office. As a Jew and a Zionist he had helped draft the Balfour Declaration and subsequently he advised the Zionists on their memorandum which was submitted to the Paris Peace Conference. Highly placed and influential, but also tactful and discreet, he was able to keep the Zionists closely informed as to the likely shape of events in government. His name

was brought up casually for the position of high commissioner
during the discussions at San Remo when the mandates were
apportioned to Britain and France. Lord Balfour's approval was
obtained while he was engaged in a tennis match with an
Italian delegate. No one seemed unduly alarmed at the possible
implications of the recent disturbances in Palestine and Sir
Herbert sailed forth to the warm applause of the Zionists, while
the Arabs received him with something far less than enthusiasm.
When he left Palestine five years later, Zionists had become
disillusioned by his even-handed treatment of the Arabs which
they called weakness and partiality. In itself, this was a tribute
to the man's administration.

5

The Horns of a Dilemma

When Britain abandoned her Mandate over Palestine in 1948, His Majesty's Government was, in effect, absolving itself of any responsibility for its future. To emphasize the point, the British delegation to the United Nations abstained from the debates and the voting on the partition of Palestine. This simple act of withdrawal could not, however, cover up Britain's role and share in creating the tragedy of modern Palestine. Power imposes its own responsibilities and the abdication of her privileged position of authority in Palestine was a result of Britain's failure to fully recognize the responsibility for the burden she had actively sought and secured.

Nearly thirty years before, from the time of Sir Herbert Samuel's civilian administration, it was clear that the first priority of the Balfour Declaration was to be the establishment of a Jewish national home. The declaration was repeated in the introduction to the mandate instrument, and none of its major articles revealed any shift of intention or alteration of this main objective. The mandate document moreover spelled out the *means* by which the national home policy could be implemented. A Jewish agency, that is, an arm of the World Zionist Organization, would advise and cooperate with the British administration in Palestine in all matters, social, political and economic, which would affect the establishment of the Jewish National Home. The British administration would facilitate Jewish immigration and the settlement of Jews on the land. These arrangements were settled through mutual consultation and, like the Balfour Declaration, the mandate document was co-authored by British officials and the Zionists.

Committed to the National Home, Britain also had to face the reality of articulate Palestinian opposition to both her

presence and her policy. The time had come to admit that the
"non-Jewish" elements of the population were a more tangible
factor than the as yet non-existent Jewish population of the
National Home. It was evident from the beginning that large-
scale Jewish immigration would ultimately lead to an attempt to
found a Jewish state. Sir Herbert Samuel had observed before he
became Palestine's first high commissioner that the *immediate*
creation of a Jewish state would be undemocratic since a minority
would rule a majority. Therefore conditions must be fulfilled,
including large-scale immigration, he said, in order that "with
the minimum of delay the country may become a purely self-
governing commonwealth under an established Jewish majority."[11]

Palestinians read the fine print of the mandate policy and it
was inconceivable that they would meekly accept the emasculation
of the Arab identity of their own land. They had heard an
earlier appeal from King Hussein who reminded them that their
sacred books and traditions placed upon them the duties of
hospitality and tolerance. "Welcome the Jews as brethren,"
Hussein had said, "and cooperate with them for the common
welfare." When Weizmann spoke in Jerusalem to an assembly
of Palestinian notables about a cultural and spiritual home for
the Jews, one Arab dignitary replied in the words of the famous
Muslim tradition: "Your rights are our rights and our obligations
are yours."

The essence of the Zionist movement appeared to most
Palestinians, however, to be far removed from spiritual values.
They thought it best expressed in the words of Jacob Klatzkin,
a Zionist theorist, who wrote: "In longing for our land we do not
desire to create in Palestine a base for the spiritual values of
Judaism. To regain our land is for us an end in itself. Our basic
intention, whether consciously or unconsciously, is to deny any
conception of Jewish identity based on spiritual values."[12]

Jewish nationalism, therefore, had to be countered on political
grounds. Muslim-Christian associations were formed with openly
declared political objectives. The associations had appealed in vain
to the Paris Peace Conference to allow a Palestinian representative
to attend their deliberations. Now an Arab congress was convened
in Haifa (December 1921) at which an Arab executive was
elected to take the Palestinians' protests directly to the British.

A second and more serious outbreak of violence had occurred the previous May in Jaffa when Jews were attacked at the government immigration offices. The violence spread to neighboring Jewish settlements and the toll of dead was heavy. The congress sought the abolition of the national home policy, and the formation of a representative national government to direct the affairs of Palestine. The tactics of the congress were to urge radical changes in the proposed terms of the Mandate before it was ratified, in order to protect the rights and interests of 90 percent of the population.

The demands of the congress were rejected by the British colonial secretary, Winston Churchill. Despite his assurances that the obligations entrusted to Britain under the Mandate would be fulfilled with absolute impartiality, the congress was by then fully aware that the Mandate itself was conceived in a partisan spirit. The question of Jewish immigration was central, for the Zionist control of immigration had sparked the Jaffa riots. The Arabs believed that the democratic right of self-government would not be granted until such time as the Jews constituted a majority in the country. Churchill did nothing to discourage this belief.[13]

The British Government had worked itself onto the horns of a nasty dilemma. As mandatory power only two genuine alternatives lay before it: *either* cut off Jewish immigration at a level where the Jews would not be strong enough to aim at or seize statehood, *or* take decisive steps toward the establishment of a Jewish state and accomplish that task before Arab opposition became strong enough to check developments. Either there would be a Jewish state or there would not: it was a situation which Shakespeare's Hamlet would have appreciated.

The official attitude of His Majesty's Government, apart from any private misgivings of individual ministers, was to maintain the stance of impartiality toward both Zionists and Palestinians. Two equal obligations were imposed upon the government: one was to create suitable conditions for the establishment of the Jewish National Home and the other to safeguard the rights of the Arab (the so-called "non-Jewish") population.

At the time this must have seemed the most realistic course to adopt, but translated into policy it was inherently more dangerous than either of the other mutually exclusive alternatives. A declaration of equal obligations was susceptible to attack from two sides. Both the Zionists and the Arabs could, and frequently did, charge Britain with failing to fulfill their own particular part of the bargain. Far more dangerous still was the simple fact that the policy rested on an unrealistic premise. It assumed that, in return for a verbal pledge safeguarding civil and religious rights, the Palestinians, as a people, would submit without question or discussion to a scheme which they had had no hand in creating; that they would, moreover, acquiesce to this scheme which would fundamentally alter the political character of their society, if not extinguish them altogether as a community, *as though that scheme in no way concerned them.*

British policy makers continually viewed the two "obligations" as entirely unrelated to each other. If, however, as events were to prove, fulfilling the one resulted in the impossibility of fulfilling the other, then one obligation was indeed intimately connected with the other.

The Haycraft Commission which investigated the causes of the Jaffa riots naïvely declared that the hostility between the two races, the Jews and the Arabs, could be eased if both sides were prepared to discuss their problems in a reasonable spirit. The basis for such discussion, however, would be that "the Arabs should accept implicitly the declared policy of the government on the subject of the Jewish National Home, and that the Zionist leaders should abandon and repudiate all pretensions that go beyond it."

"What the British were trying to do at the time," a former Jordanian cabinet minister (now living in Jerusalem and therefore requesting anonymity) told me immediately after the Six Day War, "was to offer us a poison brew of their own concoction, assuring us at the same time that the Zionists would not shoot us. In either case we were doomed." He smiled wryly and added: "Today, the Israelis don't say they will shoot us; instead they annex our whole city and then exile our leaders."

The assumption that a dual obligation did exist provided a satisfying interpretation of the political history of the Mandate as simply the struggle between two irreconcilable nationalisms, Jewish and Arab. British observers found this useful for it moved the burden of responsibility for the course and ultimate failure of the Mandate from the shoulders of the mandatory power onto the backs of the two contending parties. The analysis had other ramifications which Zionists seized on. Since the conflict involved only Arab and Jew, then only they could find the solution to it. This bilateral responsibility was then neatly halved by making the basis for a solution the *Palestinians'* acceptance of the British policy of the Jewish National Home.

The argument had an almost mystical allure for the liberal mind because of its appeal to "reason." And so, when the Palestinian rejects British policy, and thereby the basis for a solution to the Arab-Jewish conflict, he is accused of being unreasonable and irrational. Finally, when this improbable syllogism has worked itself out, the Arab is blamed for the failure of a policy which he has not contrived and of a scheme on which he has not been consulted. While it is true that the relationship between the Zionists and the Palestinians aggravated an already difficult situation, the imperialist relationship between Britain and the Arabs was one of power to powerlessness. The official claim of equal obligations was, in the final analysis, an illusion. Consequently, British policy was unintelligible to the very people whom it was intended to convince.

A second Arab congress met in Jerusalem in May 1921. The congress decided to send a delegation to London to campaign against Britain's mandate policy. It was headed by a former mayor of Jerusalem. Musa Kazem Husseini, a venerated patriarch of moderate views and disposition. The Palestinians urged the British Government to introduce a legislative council representative of *all* the people of Palestine including, of course, the present Jewish inhabitants.

A draft constitution was accordingly published in February 1922 by His Majesty's Government, whereby the government would be entrusted to an official executive and a legislative council. The senior executive and commander in chief was the high commissioner who was empowered to give effect to the provisions of the Mandate, namely, the establishment of the Jewish National Home. The legislative council would comprise, in addition to the high commissioner, ten official and twelve non-official members. The officials were to be appointed by the high

Several actions of the Palestinians demonstrated a willingness to work together but all suggestions/ attempts were rejected /shot down commissioner and would be exclusively British. The non-official members would be elected: eight from the Muslim community, two from the Christian (Arab) and two from the Jewish.

The proposed constitution was a bitter disappointment to the Arab delegation. It was evident that with the ten official members and the two Jews, the mandate administration would have an absolute majority (twelve out of twenty-two) in the legislative council. In this way it could enforce the national home policy against the wishes of the representatives of the majority of the population. Other provisions removed all possible safeguards for the Arabs. The high commissioner had the right to veto any legislation; he could conduct the business of the council with a quorum of ten which he could always ensure with his own officials; finally, there was the provision that "no ordinance shall be passed which shall be in any way repugnant to or inconsistent with the provisions of the Mandate." This last clause, loosely interpreted, could deny any Palestinian request, legitimate or otherwise, and the council was structured in such a way as to make the denial effective.

Colonial Secretary Winston Churchill used the draft constitution in an attempt to get the Arabs to capitulate completely to the terms of the Mandate. He made it clear to the Arab delegation that the national home policy was not susceptible to change, nor was it subject to discussion. Only the method of safeguarding the Arabs' civil and religious rights was a proper subject of negotiation, and the secretary regarded the proposed legislative council as adequate. Churchill then stated that he could not negotiate *officially* with any delegation which merely "claimed" to represent the wishes of its people.[14] He urged the acceptance of the draft constitution since its object was to provide Palestinians with a "constitutional channel for the expression of their opinions and wishes." Bullshit

The Arabs were left the option of debating the details of their gradual subordination in Palestine. To accept the proposed council was to accept implicitly the national home policy, and the composition of the council would ensure its fulfillment. Confronted with this constitutional coercion, the Arab delegation felt itself forced to reject Churchill's "concessions." In effect the Arabs told the colonial secretary that "until we see a real practical change in the policy of the British Government we must harbor fears that the intention to create the Jewish National Home is to cause the disappearance or subordination of the Arabic population, culture and language in Palestine." The change never came and fears increased. The issue of a legislative council was raised on two or three other occasions, but came to nothing. Throughout the mandate period the Arab community was governed by the high commissioner and his ten British advisors. For many years two of the top executive positions, the attorney general and the director of immigration, were filled by British Jews who were also Zionists.

The British Government could only offer the Arabs paper assurances that their rights would be protected. But these protestations of goodwill were usually coupled with the thinly veiled threat that no government would ever abandon the Balfour Declaration. British authorities spoke to the Arab with a reassuring liberal voice, but always echoed the menacing commands of self-confident power. The national home policy was never justified to the Arabs beyond the claim that Britain had made a solemn promise to the Zionists. This was incomprehensible to the Palestinians, and any material advantage stemming from mandate rule and Jewish investment in the country was canceled by the multiple dimensions of the threat to the existing Arab community. Palestine was, in fact, governed like any colony of the British Empire and the high commissioner was in benevolent but autocratic command of all he surveyed. Inevitably the people became estranged from the source of authority, a situation which was an encouragement to violence since Palestinians realized they must either endure perpetual submission or break the law.

Westminster had drastically underestimated the depth of Arab feeling. Opposition to the Mandate was dismissed as the work of discontented intellectuals or disgruntled agitators. The Zionists made a similar misjudgment; they attributed the cause of violence to the machinations of upper-class landowners who were anxious to preserve their privileged position in society as well as their feudal hold over the peasantry. Both interpretations are valid only if we are prepared to turn a blind eye to what was really happening among the Arab population.

✳ The Brits really had no right to make such a promise, giving away the Palestinian's land.

It was natural that the most politically conscious groups would be the first to express their resentment to the Mandate and it was also natural that opposition would be voiced by the educated few. The members of the congress and the Arab executive were landowners and professional men. The congress abounded with the names of the educated families of the aristocracy, such as Nashashibi, Husseini, Khalidi, Dajani, Tukan and Abd al-Hadi. These leaders would be expected to arouse the population against the foreign ruler and his policy. But it was wrong to assume that peasants were incapable of political judgment or deep feeling, or that their resentment sprang merely from a cultivated religious fanaticism. Fierce Arab opposition could not be reduced to what psychologists might call the collective egoisms of the various elements of society.

The congress was the first body to express the growing sense of Arab community identity against the external threat of the national home policy. Peasant and landlord alike felt their political and material interests were identical. It was a common sight in the villages to find illiterate peasants gathered at the home of one of their educated brethren to hear the newspaper read to them, following which a lively discussion of the major issues of the day would engross all of them. In a largely illiterate society this was the only way of keeping up with the news.

This system of political discussion is as alive as ever. I was sitting some years ago in an open-air café with a group of Jordanian villagers. When they discovered I was Canadian, they bombarded me with questions about "unrest" among the French Canadians in Quebec. I explained as best I could of French desires to preserve the integrity of their culture, to run their own affairs. They were instantly sympathetic. Beside me an older man said: "Your French fight the same struggle we lost; I hope they will not be deprived of their homeland, as we have been." Not surprisingly, one Royal Commission concluded after an intensive survey of rural Palestine that "the Arab peasants and villagers are probably more politically minded than many people of Europe."[16]

Peasants and farmers were actively concerned in their

country's affairs. Peasant parties, organized mainly by lawyers, sprang up throughout Palestine in the mid-twenties. A large conference of about 1,000 farmers was held in tents near Hebron in 1929 and several resolutions were passed relating to their needs and the methods the British administration should adopt to improve their condition.

The growing nationalist movement was further supported by Arab women. In October 1929, a Palestine Arab Women's Congress was held in Jerusalem.[6] Women from all over the country presented reports to the congress on the unsatisfactory conditions in their communities. Resolutions were handed to the high commissioner, and a demonstration against the mandate policy was staged through the streets of the Holy City. It was the first time in Palestine's long history that women had indulged in political activities.

Despite widespread backing from all quarters of the population, Arab leaders realized that without some tangible form of power in Arab hands they could not hope to guide the destiny of their people. The mandatory regime, like all colonial administrations, was rigidly conservative and the British were obsessed with matters of security. Pouring money into educational facilities and social services for the Arab community was considered little better than subsidizing unrest. The government pleaded financial stringency, but at one time when schools were closed down and teachers dismissed for "lack of funds" the treasury actually showed a surplus of six million pounds on its books. Meanwhile, the Jewish community was making rapid progress in all aspects of development under the protection of British colonial rule. The status quo was being altered in their favor. Arabs had to fight on two fronts, both against the British and the Zionists. While the British excluded them from a genuine role in government planning and decision making, the Zionists simply excluded the Arabs from everything.

The Arabs' fear of Zionism was derived from its Jewish exponents in Palestine. Giving evidence before the Haycraft Commission, Dr. Eder, the acting chairman of the Zionist Commission, said that in his view of the Zionist ideal there could only be "one National Home in Palestine, and that a Jewish one, and no equality in the partnership between Jews

and Arabs, but a Jewish predominance as soon as the numbers
of that race are sufficiently increased."[7] Dr. Eder added his
belief that Jews, not Arabs, should have the right to bear arms
on the grounds that "this discrimination would tend to improve
Arab-Jewish relations."[8]

Harry Sacher, head of the Political Department of the Jewish
Agency, told the Shaw Commission in 1929 that political rights
could not be granted the Arabs if that meant the immediate
establishment of representative democratic institutions. The
leader of the Zionist revisionist wing, Vladimir Jabotinksy
argued essentially along the same lines: only when a Jewish
majority was achieved could parliamentary institutions be
introduced so that, as he candidly put it, "the Jewish point of
view should always prevail."[8a] Israel Zangwill once suggested
that the Arabs of Palestine should be resettled elsewhere in
order to liberate the land for Jewish nationalization. At about
the same time Chaim Weizmann replied to a reporter's question
concerning the problem of the Arab majority: "We expect they
won't be in a majority after a few years."[9]

These views were well known to the Arabs. The opinions of
Zionist leaders reflected the general attitude of the average
Zionist settler toward the Arab. Even the most liberal of the
Jewish pioneers would shrug his shoulders and say: "We cannot
afford to see the Arabs' point of view."[10] There was, of course,
another side to the story. The 12th Zionist Congress in Carlsbad
in 1921, passed a resolution reassuring Palestinians that the
progress of Jewish colonization would not affect their rights.
From time to time similar declarations were repeated. The
Arabs, however, could be excused for cynically dismissing such
resolutions as better suited to Zionist propaganda needs in
Europe rather than its practical ends in Palestine.

Frederick Kisch, head of the Zionist executive in Palestine,
conceded that the major weakness of the Jewish Agency was that
in its program for cooperation with the Arabs "its fine words
were not matched by deeds."[11] The small group known as
Brit Shalom, which called for a bi-national Arab-Jewish state,
was outside the mainstream of Zionist thinking and influence.
Arabs respected the members of Brit Shalom, but they knew

their real struggle would be against hard-core Zionists like Ben Gurion.

In fact, no program of cooperation could exist. It was characteristic of the single-mindedness of Zionist leaders to proclaim the universalist principles of their movement while denying their application to the Arabs of Palestine with whom they were in direct and daily contact. Outlining the imperatives of Zionism, Ben Gurion stated that Jewish nationalism was "part of a tremendous movement which involves all of humanity — the world revolution, whose aims are the redemption of man from every form of enslavement, discrimination and exploitation..."[12] But in Palestine where the Arabs struggled against the colonial rule of Britain, Zionism could hardly pretend to be part of that same struggle while claiming the protection of the Balfour Declaration and the Mandate Power.

The Jewish National Home developed along the lines of a sub-national government, a kind of state within a state. The internal affairs of the Jewish community, the Yishuv, were conducted by an elected national council. The Palestine Zionist Executive, later the Jewish Agency, provided the liaison between the mandate administration and the World Zionist Organization (W.Z.O.). The Agency drew upon the political and financial resources of the World Zionist body which functioned in most European countries and in North America. With these resources at hand, the Agency was able, through its various departments, to control efficiently the economy of the Jewish sector of Palestine, as well as build schools and hospitals, direct public works programs and exploit natural resources through government concessions such as the Palestine Electric Corporation.

As early as 1929 the Jewish community possessed its own para-military force, the Haganah, and in the last years of the Mandate an intelligence service was organized comprising Jewish officials in the Palestine Government who acted as informers. Through its connections with the W.Z.O., the Jewish community was able to exploit worldwide propaganda outlets. Zionism was never the monolithic movement it often appeared to be, but with skillful organization it had a remarkable success in shaping favorable public opinion.

One of Zionism's greatest assets was its capacity to tailor its propaganda to particular moments and specific audiences. Jew and Gentile alike were attracted for a variety of reasons: religious, humanitarian, social, imperial. Even anti-Semites found their own interests could be furthered by cooperation with the Zionists. If matters did not always go their way, Zionists were confident — with good reason — that a local setback in Palestine could be repaired in Whitehall through its many sympathizers and supporters. In contrast, as British Member of Parliament Richard Crosland put it: "The only way the Arabs can get a hearing is through violence." This was unfortunately true, but of no great help to the Arabs in the long run. Violence begets violence, and events were to show that the Arabs were far less equipped to sustain the alternative of violence than were either the British or the Zionists.

Immigration was a major priority of the Jewish Agency. Measured against Zionist aspirations, the level of immigration during the first decade was disappointingly low. Between 1920 and 1929 about 80,000 Jews entered Palestine as permanent residents, although annual figures fluctuated considerably owing to uncertain economic conditions both inside and outside the country. Measured against Arab expectations, the incoming tide of aliens did not materialize. The proportion of Jews to the total population grew from 10 percent in 1920 to 16 percent in 1931. Nevertheless, the government's immigration policy exposed the economy to certain dangers and intensified the unstable relations between Jew and Arab.

Immigration was not based on rational principles which took into account the long-range interests of the country as a whole. The only criterion used to judge the immigration level was the country's economic absorptive capacity. Social, political and psychological factors were disregarded. The most important immigrant category was the labor list. Every six months the high commissioner would place a specified number of immigration certificates at the disposal of the Zionist Organization. In applying for them Zionists tended, for propaganda purposes, to exaggerate every favorable circumstance to obtain the largest possible number of certificates.[131] As a result the government was under political pressure every six months to provide a large labor schedule. There was no time to make adjustments for the dislocations which were bound to arise from rapid increases in the population. An expert employed by the Jewish Agency in 1927 concluded that "much of the employment in the country during 1926 and 1927 was, in fact, the consequence of this hasty and unbalanced flow of Jewish immigration."[14]

Immigrants were being admitted at a time when the government was supplying relief work for Jewish laborers already in the country. At the same time the level of Arab employment or unemployment was not taken into account when drawing up the labor list. Two of the British Government's own commissions, the Shaw (1929) and the Hope Simpson (1930) advised more stringent controls of immigration. When Whitehall adopted their advice the result was tantamount to throwing a grenade into an explosives arsenal. The House of Commons witnessed an opposition onslaught on the government's new policy statement; Chaim Weizmann resigned as chief of the W.Z.O. in protest against the government's "whittling away" of the National Home. Combined pressure finally forced Prime Minister Ramsay MacDonald to explain away the proposed changes until all the whittled shavings were glued back onto the old policy plank.

The actual control of immigration was another point of Arab grievance. Effective control was not in the hands of the Palestine Government, which was ostensibly the responsible body, but held by the Zionists themselves. The selection of immigrants, their financing, settlement and allotment of funds was handled entirely by the Zionist Organization, which consequently was invested with the power, but not the corresponding responsibility, for its actions.[15] The all-important labor schedule accounted for 50 percent of total immigration: if the category of laborers' dependents is included, then the Zionists had direct and indirect control of nearly 70 percent of all immigration into Palestine. On this subject the Shaw Commission noted that Zionists seemed more concerned with the "political creed" of prospective immigrants than with their particular qualifications.

The ethical aspect of Zionism was expressed in the twin concepts of the conquest of labor and the conquest of land. The conquest of labor was accomplished through the establishment of production, marketing and service cooperatives organized by the Jewish Federation of Labor (Histadrut) which gradually

emerged as the most powerful political force in the Yishuv. The
conquest of land was accomplished through agricultural colonization, the establishment of communal settlements both by private
enterprise and by the Jewish National Fund. Land purchased by the
J.N.F. became the inalienable property of the Jewish people.
Leaders of the Jewish labor movement (the Ben Gurions and the
Ben Zvis) were inspired by universal socialist ideals, although
in practice they pursued a policy of socio-economic "apartheid"
through the exclusion of Arab labor from Jewish enterprises run
by the Histadrut and from land bought by the J.N.F.[116] A
picketing campaign was launched against private Jewish agricultural settlements where Arab labor was employed. These
were generally the older settlements where good relations had
developed between Jewish farmers and their Arab laborers. The
newspaper *Davar* described the effects of the campaign at one
settlement near Jaffa:

> A branch of the labor office has been opened in Beit Vegen.
> The office has begun an important social activity in which it has
> been helped also by the contracting office of the Workers' Council
> of Tel Aviv. During the last five months the position has changed
> as follows. In place of 200 Arab workers and 50 Jews, the last
> count gives 200 Hebrew workers and 70 Arab workers in Beit
> Vegen. The work continues.[117]

A more realistic and more genuinely socialist approach might
have been for organized Jewish labor to combine with cheap,
unorganized Arab labor to raise the general level of wages
against the combined interests of Arab and Jewish capitalists.
In any event, the Histadrut policy drove even deeper the wedge
separating Jew and Arab. In his report, Sir John Hope Simpson
criticized these practices. The exclusion of Arab labor, he said,
was incompatible with the expressed sentiments of Zionists that
they desired relations of friendship and respect with Arabs. Two
communities could not grow up in peace if the indifference of
the one fed suspicion and fear in the other. Sir John added that
the Histadrut's policy of "persistent and deliberate boycott" of
Arab labor was a continuing source of conflict in Palestine. If
Arabs accused Zionists of being alien intruders, Zionists constantly
reminded them that it was so.
Education too might have been an area in which close contacts

between Jewish and Arab youth could have dispelled the atmosphere of alienation. But again separate development was the rule. Jewish and Arab public schools (such as there were of the latter) existed apart. The Jewish school system was only nominally under the control of the Mandate Government's director of education, although it was partially financed from the government's budget. The Arab system, like all aspects of their community, was controlled directly by the government.

The mandate administration proposed the establishment of a British university in the city of Jerusalem to serve as the educational apex of the two public school systems. The Zionist executive informed Sir Ronald Storrs, the author of the scheme, that the Jews would not participate because it "constituted a threat to Hebrew culture in Palestine."[18] The project was dropped and the only university to be constructed in Palestine was the Hebrew University which, while admitting Arab students, meant that higher education, even partially in their own cultural tradition, was not available to Arabs. The Zionist executive consistently refused to have anything to do with any education program where Hebrew was not the sole language of instruction. An idea for an Arab-Jewish agricultural school was likewise shelved and instead two separate schools were established.[19]

As the wall was erected brick by brick between the Arab and Jewish communities, events dragged each side of the political triangle toward the precipice, and over the edge into an abyss of prolonged and violent encounter. Zionists claimed that neither Arab nor Jew should dominate the other, but their actions and policies would lead them logically to seize control of Palestine. Britain originally intended to govern two peoples impartially; but its policy was to allow the Jews wide latitude for development while ruling rather than governing the Arab community. When the crisis came between Britain and the Arabs, Britain opted for repression instead of concession. The Arabs were being asked to accept a European concept of a just solution to its own Jewish problem: in fact the Arabs were being forced to submit to the inequitable consequences of that solution. Sovereignty was a question of destiny and the Arab in his own land could not concede that the reins of his destiny be held forever by foreign hands. Zionists read the future in the same light.

6

The Arab Rebellion 1936-1938

The early nineteen-thirties were prosperous ones for Palestine, the more remarkable by contrast with the depression into which the world as a whole was plunged. With the expansion of industry and agriculture Jewish immigration increased dramatically. In 1930 the figure was 4,944 immigrants; in 1932, 9,553; in 1933, 30,327; in 1934, 42,359; and in 1935, 61,854. By 1936 Jews comprised 30 percent of the total population. Illegal immigration was on the upswing and any number of ingenious methods were used to bring Jews to the Promised Land. There is the story of enterprising young Palestinian Jewish men who became professional husbands, "marrying" single girls in Europe who wanted easy access to Palestine, "divorcing" them with a handshake once the ship had docked in Haifa.[11]

Nineteen thirty-three began as any other year, but three apparently unrelated incidents, none of them earthshaking on the surface, seemed to portend the tumultuous years which lay ahead. A man died. In the Jewish community elections were held. The high commissioner made a proposal.

When Musa Kazem Husseini died, his moderating influence on the Arab political movement disappeared as well. Respected and accepted by all factions, Musa had led several delegations to England to urge the colonial office to grant representative institutions to Palestine.

With his death the nationalist movement passed completely into the hands of Hajj Amin Husseini, head of the Supreme Muslim Council and Mufti of Jerusalem. A man of medium stature, bearded, and with gentle eyes which concealed a tough and uncompromising disposition, Hajj Amin had received the traditional Muslim education at the Azhar University in Cairo.

His talents were as political as religious for he had been from youth an ardent nationalist. In 1918 he cooperated with the British Army, raising some 2,000 recruits in Palestine in the belief that the Allied promises to the Arabs would be fulfilled. Two years later he was strongly attacking the Zionist policies of the British. Accused of fomenting the 1920 disturbances, Hajj Amin was sentenced to ten years in exile.

High Commissioner Sir Herbert Samuel later pardoned Hajj Amin and appointed him head of the Supreme Muslim Council, which curiously earned him the tag among some Arab elements of being a British agent. The Mufti's bitter attitude toward Britain was accentuated by the disillusionment caused by Prime Minister Ramsay MacDonald's retreat from the recommendations of his own commissions on Palestine which had become short-lived government policy in the White Paper of 1930.

Hajj Amin Husseini now concluded that organized resistance to the Mandate was the only means of bringing about meaningful concessions for the Arabs. He actively discouraged the sale of land to Jews, and the Muslim Supreme Council purchased land in competition with the Jewish National Fund. He also encouraged greater expenditure on education in Muslim religious schools controlled by the Council: 19 percent of its budget was tied up in education as compared to a meager 5 percent allocated by the mandate government from its revenues for the entire country. During the Arab rebellion of 1936-1938 Hajj Amin ruthlessly eliminated his political opponents who advocated a more moderate line with the British. In the long run this was a tactical blunder, for when the rebellion was crushed by the British and the Mufti himself banished forever from Palestine, no effective leadership remained inside the country and the Arab nationalist resistance collapsed.

The second incident was the election in the Jewish community in which the labor group of the Histadrut led by Ben Gurion captured control of the Jewish Agency. It was natural to expect a shift in Zionist strategy from the gradualist approach to Jewish statehood. Zionists believed that the Arabs were no longer

strong enough to destroy the position of the Jewish community.
The next stage of their strategy was, therefore, to ensure that
the relationship of Jewish and Arab forces was such as to
preclude the possibility of establishing an Arab state in Palestine.
Once the Arabs were unable to frustrate the growth of the Jewish
community, then a solution could be reached based upon the
premise of effective power being in the hands of the Jews. This,
however, required a transition period during which the Jewish
minority would exercise organized revolutionary rule over the
whole country. The idea was that the state apparatus, the
administration and the military establishment would fall into
their hands.[12]

Zionists had at last accepted the logic of their scheme for
the National Home which would put them on a collision course
with the Arabs. The principle of minority rule had previously
been rejected, but once granted it became linked with a
territorial imperative which implied that the National Home
could be Jewish only if the removal of a major part, or all of the
Arab population were accomplished. Then the control of the
state would pass legitimately into the hands of the majority.

In 1933 the high commissioner, Sir Arthur Wauchope,
advocated self-determination by stages for all of Palestine. The
final stage called for a legislative council. The details of its
composition revealed that the Arabs would have fourteen of
twenty-eight seats which ensured the Arab community a greater
measure of security than previous proposals. The Arab leaders
decided to discuss the question and sent a delegation to London
in January 1936, led by Hajj Amin Husseini, who was skeptical
of the outcome. The plan had already been denounced by the
Zionist Congress in Lucerne, Switzerland, and the Jewish Agency
followed suit. In both Houses of Parliament the council scheme
was bitterly attacked. The British Government again retreated
under pressure, and the plan was withdrawn.

Arab reaction was predictable. No one doubted that the
Zionist lobby in London had caused the council proposal to be
dropped.

A new element entered the confused picture when a cache
of arms consigned to an unidentified Jew were found in barrels
of cement at the port of Jaffa. Two thirds of the cement

consignment contained a total of 800 rifles and revolvers and an estimated 500,000 rounds of ammunition.

Rumors spread that the Zionist settlements were arming against the Arabs. The peasantry was restive and a spirit of rebellion moved swiftly among them. One Izzadin Qassam acted. Soon there were tales out of the hills of Galilee of the exploits of this romantic figure who led a small band of guerillas against armed Jewish settlements and British garrisons. He scored several successes in about eight months of guerilla activity, harassing armed Jewish camps and even British forts. For the embattled Palestinians he symbolized a love of liberty, a scorn of death, a fresh breeze of idealistic faith and vigor which fanned the smoldering embers of revolt. The British hunted him down as a worthless brigand. Instead he suffered a martyr's death at the hands of his country's oppressors and was mourned by Arabs throughout Palestine.

In April 1936, serious riots erupted in Jaffa in the course of which sixteen Jews and five Arabs were killed. Recently established Arab political parties immediately formed a united front known as the Arab Higher Committee under the leadership of Hajj Amin Husseini. The committee was made up of members from all party factions as well as both religions, Christian and Muslim. It summoned the Arabs to a nationwide strike against the Mandate in order to bring an end to Jewish immigration, land sales to the Jewish National Fund, and finally to bring about the creation of a national government responsible to a representative council. These remained the minimum safeguards for the protection of the Arab community. The high commissioner reacted quickly, enacting drastic regulations, including a curfew, censorship, search-and-arrest-without-warrant and deportation for political undesirables.

The strike began nevertheless as an economic boycott against the Jewish community. Shops in the cities and towns were shuttered and silent.[131] The streets filled with crowds of demonstrators demanding justice for their people and the police were called in to disband them by force. In Nazareth an angry crowd stoned a police contingent which then turned on the demonstrators supported by armed members of the British Loyal Regiment.

The next day at the Damascus Gate in Old Jerusalem, Arab

students armed with sticks attacked police near the government offices. The police charged in a flying wedge wielding batons and drove the students into the narrow winding streets of the walled city. A shot fired from a cafe by an unknown assailant felled one policeman. The story was the same in Haifa, Ramleh and Hebron. The district commissioner's office in Gaza was stoned while the population barricaded the main streets for protection against the police and soldiers, who were equipped with Lewis automatic weapons and tear gas.

On May 26 a lively fusillade rang through the night in the gardens and orange groves around Jaffa as soldiers and Arabs engaged each other in a deadly caricature of hide-and-seek. Jaffa continued to defy any pacification attempts by the authorities. The tough and rugged Jaffa boatmen lived in the mass of closely packed houses perched above the port; by day they pelted police patrols with bombs, then vanished among the labyrinth of narrow lanes.

The young men then left the streets to their sisters and elders. They slipped into the hills to join their cousins from the villages who had formed guerilla bands. There was no central organization and yet guerillas sprang up all over Palestine. They had no real knowledge of guerilla tactics yet they blew up bridges in the south, derailed trains at Nablus and Tulkarm, attacked British convoys wherever they were encountered and even shot down an airplane whose pilot was imprudent enough to attempt a ground-level bombing attack. These incidents began to assume the aspects of the Irish Easter Rebellion and, like the Irish, the Arabs were up against the British Empire itself. The British garrison had doubled before the end of May, and redoubled before June was out. Famous regiments like the Cameron and Seaforth Highlanders were transferred to Palestine in battalion strength. Thousands of troops combed the hills for dissidents and R.A.F. fighter planes bombed and strafed the hills where guerillas were suspected of hiding.

The high commissioner took further security measures and increased the penalties for bomb throwing, for firing on soldiers and for the illegal possession of weapons. Collective punishments were imposed on whole towns and villages. In the working-class quarter of Jaffa, 237 tenement houses were blown up on the pretext of initiating a town-planning scheme, thereby increasing the hardships of the growing urban proletariat. House to house searches for guns and ammunition were conducted in the Arab villages. At one location, Kefr Kenna, village women stoned the troops from the rooftops of their homes. The soldiers replied with Lewis guns; miraculously only a young girl of nine was killed.

The secretary-general of the Arab Higher Committee, Auni Abdul Hadi, and forty-nine prominent labor and strike leaders were arrested and interned in a camp on the Egyptian frontier where they promptly set about sabotaging the camp's installations provoking more severe security measures against them. The Arab Higher Committee issued a manifesto urging the non-payment of taxes on the principle of "no taxation without representation." At the same time the committee issued a statement eschewing violence in all forms, claiming that the object of the strike was to recover the Arabs' violated rights. Unorganized and undirected, the violence increased.

There was, however, a lighter side to the wave of unrest. One evening the police received a telephone call from a village near Jerusalem. Two *fellah* had found a Jew wandering in the hills and the villagers wanted the police to come and collect him. The young man, perplexed at having been led to the village and locked in a room, explained to the police that he had been enjoying his customary nocturnal stroll. In the circumstances, the Arab villagers had decided the man must be mad and in his distraught state of mind the confines of a police barracks would be safer for him.

The war of nerves between the high commissioner and the Arab Higher Committee continued through the long, hot Palestinian summer. A large number of labor certificates had been issued to the Jewish Agency in May at the same time as the announcement of another Royal Commission to investigate the causes of the "disturbances." The British Government insisted that the strike end before the commissioners were sent to Palestine, and the Higher Committee demanded at least the

cessation of Jewish immigration as a condition for an end to the
resistance.

After six months the strike had a telling effect on the Arab
community, which could no longer finance the shutdown of the
economy. Moreover, it was evident that the guerillas were no
match for the superior British forces. The Higher Committee was
driven to the wall, and in October the strike was broken without
it having won a single concession. The rulers of Iraq, Transjordan
and Saudi Arabia had all urged the Arabs of Palestine to end
the disorders and trust the good intentions of Great Britain
which, they said, "has declared that she will do justice." In
November the Royal Commission arrived, spent three months
in Palestine and a further six months preparing its report. For
nine months an uneasy calm settled over the Holy Land.

The commission's report was issued in July 1937, simultaneously
with a Government White Paper adopting the general findings
of the report. Its main conclusion was simple: the Palestine
Mandate was unworkable. The reason was equally simple:
British obligations to the Jews could only be fulfilled by a policy
of repression against a resentful Arab population. After twenty
years of frustration and indecision the government was forced to
concede that there was "an irreconcilable conflict between the
aspirations of the Jews and Arabs in Palestine."

It was cold comfort to the Arabs that they had finally scored a
point. The commission's decision for a permanent solution to the
impasse was that Palestine should be partitioned into sovereign
Jewish and Arab states, and a British mandatory zone. The Jewish
'state would comprise the coastal plain from a point south of
Jaffa, thence to Haifa, the whole of Galilee and to the Jezreel
Valley. Jaffa would be included in the Arab state which would
comprise the rest of Palestine. The mandate zone was designed
to include the Holy Places in Jerusalem and Bethlehem, with
a corridor leading to the sea.

The concept of partition was consistently rejected by the
Arabs for the reason that it was highly prejudicial to their
interests. In the first place, the most fertile and developed part
of Palestine would fall into the area allotted to the Jewish state
where Arabs held title to four times as much land as the Jews,
and where seven-eighths of the Arab-owned citrus groves were

located. Moreover, the area remaining to the Arab state could never be economically viable. Jaffa would be isolated and a large proportion of Arabs would be placed under Jewish rule.

At the same time the majority of Zionist leaders realized that the formation of a Jewish state in only a part of Palestine and the establishment of an economically backward Arab state adjacent to it was the best means of eventually achieving their aim of a Jewish state in all of Palestine. At the 20th Zionist Congress in Zurich, Ben Gurion had said: "No Zionist can forego the smallest portion of the Land of Israel. Our debate here concerns which of two routes would lead quicker to the common goal." The Zionists anticipated the partition of Palestine and in order to enlarge their territorial claims, armed Jewish settlements — with the help of the Haganah — were being established at the rate of one a month during the course of the Arab rebellion.

Nor did partition extract Great Britain from the horns of the dilemma which it had devised for itself with the Balfour Declaration. The scheme involved the same mutually exclusive alternatives the existence of which the government had denied by professing itself impartially committed to an equal obligation to both Arab and Jew. Professor Hourani has observed that partition was not a middle solution, but in fact a pro-Jewish solution, since, he says: "It conceded the essence of the Jewish claims, although on a smaller scale than they demanded. It involved exactly the same danger to the Arabs, and not even on a smaller scale, since if the Jews once got a foothold it would be difficult to stop them expanding."[4]

A member of the Royal Commission, Sir Laurie Hammond, committed an indiscretion when he said in May 1938, that if the Jews could get sufficient land to meet the immediate requirements of a sovereign power then this would be the first step toward getting back the rest of the country. "It will take many years," he said, "but it will come."[5]

Meanwhile, sporadic Arab resistance was resumed late in the summer of 1937 and the situation once again threatened to deteriorate. The British Government had yet to take a final decision on partition and appointed a technical team to investigate its feasibility. Then came the breaking point.

One morning in September outside a church in Nazareth,

L.Y. Andrews, district commissioner for Galilee, was shot down by four armed men. For weeks the mandate administration had been under pressure from the Jewish Agency and its supporters in England to crack down on the Arab Higher Committee and hold it responsible for the disorders. Popular sentiment against the British, however, was by then too widespread and bitter for the Higher Committee to control it, even had it been so inclined. Nevertheless, Hajj Amin issued a communiqué on the evening of Andrews' murder denouncing it as a senseless, brutal act, which it was since Andrews had been a close friend of a member of the Higher Committee and was respected by the Arab leaders.

Although the Committee was in no way connected with the deed, the administration decided to use the incident as a test of its authority. In a few days some 300 known supporters of the Supreme Muslim Council were arrested and detained while the Higher Committee was declared illegal and dissolved. Members who were caught were deported to the Seychelles. Hajj Amin succeeded in reaching the coast in disguise. A small fishing craft took him to safety in Lebanon. When disorders erupted throughout the country in protest against the wholesale removal of the Arab leaders, the government replied by imposing heavy fines on villages, indiscriminately dynamiting homes and arresting notables and villagers until some 800 prisoners were interned in camps. A few were summarily tried and executed. Of the condemned, one is still remembered today by Palestinians for the lyrics he recited extemporaneously to a fellow inmate the night before he met his death on the gallows:

> Night: let the captive finish his song;
> by dawn his wing shall flutter
> and the hanged one will swing
> in the wind.

> Night: slow your pace
> let me pour out my heart to you;
> perhaps you forgot who I am
> and what my troubles are.

> Pity how my hours have slipped
> through your hands;

> do not think I weep from fear,
> my tears are for my country...

British army engineers and Jewish laborers worked through the following winter to seal off northern Palestine from neighboring Syria from which the rebels were smuggling arms. A military road was constructed, backed by a system of barbed-wire barriers and supporting defense works. Just as Hadrian's Wall had not kept the barbarian out of England, so rebels managed to filter through the gaps in the frontier lines and melt into anonymity among the friendly and sympathetic village population.

Rebel activity redoubled in the summer of 1938 and well into the fall. In several centers the civil authorities were driven out, police stations destroyed and government offices occupied. Hebron, Beersheba, Jericho, Bethlehem, Ramallah and finally the Old City of Jerusalem felt the direct influence of the insurgents' presence. Then, as superior numbers, training and equipment began to stem the tide of rebellion, the nationalist sub-war spent itself. At the end of the fighting the British had nearly 20,000 troops in Palestine, including eighteen infantry battalions, armored cars and cavalry units, and 700 Royal Air Force personnel. Over 5,000 Arabs died in the fighting. Some 2,000 were wounded and nearly 2,500 were under detention.

The Arab nationalist movement in Palestine collapsed, and was never fully to recover.

Arab leaders were forced to ask themselves what three long years of bitter resistance had accomplished. For the sake of their future they might also have asked themselves *why* they had failed. Despite the common national goal shared alike by the workers and peasants and the upper classes of landowners and religious elite, the Palestinians could not put an end to the scheme for the Jewish National Home. Apart from the structure of the Mandate which favored the rapid growth of the Jewish community over that of the Arab majority, the failure of the nationalist movement can be explained as well by the different perspectives of the Palestinian upper class and the masses.

The upper class, represented by families like the Husseinis and the Nashishibis, sought to resolve the question of political power. Who was to rule Palestine, the British, the Arabs or the Zionists? Representative democratic institutions would not only have secured the independence of the Palestinian community from the danger of the other two fronts, but would also have served the interests of the Arab upper class which would enjoy the privilege of ruling an independent Palestine. Hence the constant efforts by the Arab leadership to negotiate directly with the British for a democratic constitution.

The reaction of the Palestinian masses in 1929 and again in 1936-1938 was not simply due to an oppressive mandate policy. It also reflected the failure of the Arab leadership to secure from the British meaningful concessions which would have alleviated the increasingly desperate situation of the peasantry. Hence the basis of political action for the masses was incoherent violence. But this violence, welling up from the bottom strata of society, terrified even the Arab leadership since it threatened to sweep them away with the tide as well. In the latest crisis, the Arab leadership tried to soothe the anger of the masses by claiming that Britain would at last recognize the justice of their cause. The failure of the nationalist movement was, in fact, due as much to the inability or unwillingness of the leadership to co-opt the full support of the masses in bringing about the destruction of the Mandate. The effendis could not think in terms of being obligated to the lower classes in the context of a total national struggle. They could only feel some obligation for the lower classes insofar as this did not conflict with their own vital interests.

The full potential of the masses was never exploited by the leadership. The real significance of this failure was not grasped by the Palestinians until after two decades of malignant despair when the Palestinian guerilla groups appeared on the scene to attempt to put together the shattered remnants of their nation.

Meanwhile, Britain had in fact officially acknowledged the implications of its mandate policy and its devastating effect on the Arab community. The partition scheme, too, was officially discarded as impractical owing to the political, administrative and financial difficulties it involved. The moment required a fresh approach to the Palestine Problem — a moment when the world was now poised precariously between war and "peace in our time."

The Arab rebellion had given the entire mandate question world prominence. For the first time Arab governments became involved on the side of the Palestinians both as a moderating force on the local situation and as a pressure on Britain to modify its policy. Fascist Italy engaged in an anti-British propaganda campaign directed at keeping Arab disaffection in Palestine alive. Germany also found the prospects attractive in playing the same game, hoping to weaken the British position in the Middle East. Moreover, however distrustful Palestinians might have been of Germany and Italy *qua* European powers, there emerged a sympathy for Germany as the ideal of a strong and unified nation which shared with the Palestinians a common enemy in Britain, and by extension also the Jews.

The area, however, was too crucial for Britain to allow it to go by default and not make some genuine gesture toward meeting fundamental Arab demands in Palestine. If war broke out in Europe, Arab friendship in the Middle East would be a useful asset, just as it had been in World War I. Against the background of the prevailing international situation, and based upon the conclusions of the most recent of its commissions, the British Government announced its new policy for Palestine in the White Paper of 1939.

The White Paper ruled out the possibility of either an Arab or a Jewish state. The constitutional solution was rather to be found in a Palestinian state in which both peoples would exercise governmental authority; a constitution drafted by Arab, Jewish and British representatives would have to provide for, among other matters, safeguards for the special position of the Jewish National Home. It was envisaged that independence could be achieved in ten years, but it was *conditional upon the development of good relations between the Arab and Jewish communities.* Both Jewish immigration and land purchases were to be subject to restrictions. The level of immigration was placed at an annual high of 15,000 for a period of five years, of which one third was to constitute a contribution toward the solution of the Jewish refugee problem in Europe. After the five years had elapsed, Arab consent to further immigration would have to be obtained. In addition land sales to Jews were restricted in certain areas, prohibited in others.

Most Arab leaders acknowledged that the White Paper went a long way toward removing the threat to Arab national existence in Palestine by ensuring (in theory at least) that a Jewish majority would never be established. There remained, however, a deep-seated suspicion that the policy would be whittled away under pressure from Zionists and their parliamentary sympathizers as had happened all too frequently in the past. For this reason Palestinians were ambivalent in their reactions to the White Paper.

The Jewish Agency on the other hand rejected the government's announcement in the strongest terms as a moral breach of the Mandate, and an illegal abandonment of the national home policy. Zionists vowed never to submit to its provisions, nor permit its implementation. It was, however, Viscount Samuel (formerly Sir Herbert Samuel, the first high commissioner to Palestine), who put his finger squarely on the weakness of the White Paper. Arab sovereignty, he observed, was subject after ten years to Jewish consent, just as further Jewish immigration was subject to Arab consent after five years. Each side was therefore given a veto on the aspirations of the other side and this was supposed to induce each to become friends. Lord Samuel concluded that the British Government apparently assumed that two negatives made a positive, rather than admit that the veto would cripple the whole scheme.

Although Palestinian Arabs had secured certain concessions from Britain, it was far from certain that the concessions were firmly secured. They had paid a heavy price for the new policy. The national movement was in total disrepair, its leaders either deported or under detention. In the early years of World War II, Britain encouraged political émigrés to return to Palestine, but only so they could be kept under close scrutiny and within reach of the authorities. The Supreme Muslim Council fell under complete British supervision. Arabic newspapers were in financial straits and many folded; those which survived suddenly switched to pro-British editorializing, which suggested they were receiving not only government encouragement, but financing as well.

Hajj Amin Husseini was forced to remain outside the country

and spent the war years trying to keep out of reach of the Allied armies. He finally wound up in Germany where he was permitted to meet Hitler and other Nazi leaders. He had reestablished the Arab Higher Committee in Beirut and Damascus and continued to claim that he was speaking in the name of the Palestinian people. He had a considerable following among the Arab masses, but his absence from the local political scene made it difficult for his own Palestine Arab Party to rebuild itself. The National Defense Party of the rival Nashishibi faction was more moderate and prepared to cooperate with Britain on the basis of the White Paper. The mandate administration for its part made no effort to cultivate moderate Arab political opinion for, having already crushed the national uprising, it preferred to take the initiative in Arab affairs and keep the political movements weak. The N.D.P. virtually collapsed after 1941 and the field was left to the smaller and less influential Istiqlal party, which was in any case unable to impose its will on the Arab community.

7

The Zionist Counterinitiative

The option of violence had failed. Twenty years of political
struggle culminating in open rebellion had brought the country
no closer to independence. By the outbreak of World War II,
Palestinians were physically and morally exhausted and the
country was beset by a crippling economic depression.

The common denominator of Arab sentiment throughout
most of the Middle East by the fall of 1939 was anti-Western,
directed especially against Britain and France, the dominating
powers in the area for two decades. In Palestine, Arabs had
experienced the sustained efforts of the British to aid a foreign
people to possess their country. It was impossible, psychologically,
for Palestinians to perform a sudden volte-face and embrace
the Allied cause in the war. Indeed, Nazi propaganda beamed
to the Arab world was effective in Palestine for the simple reason
that Germany was the declared enemy of Britain and France.
Moreover, while Britain and France had, in Arab eyes, made
a mockery of its "sacred trust of civilization," Germany had not
been tainted by the same brush. Many regarded Germany as
a potential liberator, especially as the early devastating defeats
of the Allied forces seemed to herald a Nazi sweep of Europe and
North Africa. Some shrewder minds, however, counseled caution
for fear of trading one master for another. But there were few
who paused to consider that Hitler's diabolical persecution of
Jews would force the Zionists to desperate decisions which
would make them even more determined to push their aims to
fulfillment.

Finally, despite the inevitable community of feeling between
the Arabs and Germany, the moment came when the decisive
choice had to be made. By 1942 some 9,000 Palestinian Arabs
had volunteered for the British Armed Forces, some of whom

served actively in Greece and Italy. Palestinians generally had now committed themselves to the Allied war effort.

On the national front, however, little progress was achieved. Owing to the absence of political leadership and factional disputes, Palestinians tended to look to neighboring states for guidance and support. A movement toward Arab unity, strongly supported by Britain, gained momentum in the last stages of the war. In September-October 1944, a general conference of Arab states (including Iraq, Transjordan, Saudi Arabia, Lebanon, Syria and Yemen) met in Alexandria. The outcome was a protocol which led to the founding of the Arab League in the following year. From that time on, major political decisions concerning Arab tactics against the Zionists were taken in Cairo. This development undoubtedly gave the Palestinians an important outlet through which their views reached world opinion, but it did nothing concrete by way of strengthening their community or making it more cohesive. When the final show of strength came, as it was bound to, the Jewish community was far better prepared to seize the option of violence and make it count decisively.

Indeed, the lesson of violence had not been lost on the Zionists. Force would not be discounted if the National Home could not be achieved by political means, and force would be resorted to if and when there occurred a complete breakdown in relations between Britain and the Zionists. In the end, Zionist military tactics skillfully combined with political strategy, weakened Britain's will to govern Palestine. Once Britain resolved to turn Palestine over to the United Nations for disposal, a situation was created in which force alone determined the solution vis-à-vis the Arab population. Zionists had recently accepted the implications of this challenge while, paradoxically, the Arabs who had for a long time correctly read the implications of the Zionist program failed to respond to the challenge.

Ironically, it was the British who gave the Jewish Agency the opportunity to acquire invaluable experience in the military tactics which the Zionists were to employ in undermining mandate rule. During the Arab rebellion the Mandate Government permitted the enlargement of the Jewish Settlement Police, which it also equipped and nominally placed under its control. However, the J.S.P. was largely comprised of volunteers from the Haganah, the illegal military arm of the Jewish Agency. Consequently, a legally recognized civil police force was used as a cover for the purposes of an illegal military command.

In May 1938, Orde Wingate, an Englishman with passionate Zionist leanings, organized special night squads of British and Jewish units. Under his brilliant leadership the Haganah received expert training in the latest techniques of guerilla warfare.[1] Haganah volunteers took part in offensive actions against Arab resistance fighters and Wingate's squads operated effectively in such maneuvers alongside British troops in the Galilee region.

In 1941, the Haganah set up an elite commando force called the Palmach. When Britain feared a possible German attack on Palestine, some 600 Palmach members were specially trained by a British military mission to meet this eventuality. The membership of the Haganah numbered about 21,000 men and women in 1937; by 1944 the number had risen sharply to around 37,000, many of whom had seen active service in the Allied armies during the war. It was in September of the same year that the British War Office decided to create a Jewish brigade, actually the result of persistent and repeated Zionist demands for their own fighting units to assist the Allied cause. The Jews of Palestine naturally had no alternative but to join the struggle, in whatever capacity, against the specter of Nazism devouring Europe.

A Jewish fighting force served Zionism in two ways. *First*, the brigade fought in Italy under its own banner (the Star of David which later became the flag of Israel) representing for the Jewish people an important political move toward the recognition of the principle of Jewish statehood. *Second*, as Arthur Koestler notes, the veterans of the Jewish brigade "became the nucleus of the future Israeli Army and a decisive factor in the Arab defeat which amounted to a defeat of British policy."[2] The wartime years had transformed Haganah from an informal home guard into an underground Jewish national army.

The immediate political aim of the Jewish Agency was to bring an end to the restrictions on Jewish immigration and land purchases imposed by the 1939 White Paper. The ultimate goal was set forth by David Ben Gurion, then chairman of the Jewish Agency executive, at a meeting of Zionists at the Biltmore Hotel,

New York, in May 1942. Ben Gurion dismissed any scheme
for a bi-national state if this meant offering Arabs equal
representation in the government of Palestine. The Biltmore
Conference reiterated the basic clarity of purpose always present
in political Zionism: the overriding concern of Herzl's Basle
program to which all else was subordinated, namely the establishment of Palestine as the Jewish Commonwealth. i.e. the Jewish
State. The conference also marked the beginning of an intense
campaign to enlist the support of American public opinion and
the political leaders of both the Republican and Democratic
parties to this end.

   In Palestine meanwhile the frustration and bitterness of the
Jewish community was mounting against Britain as the provisions
of the White Paper were implemented. Illegal immigration was a
means of striking a blow to redress the situation. This was, in
fact, the chief feature of Jewish activism in Palestine throughout
the war. A Committee on Illegal Immigration (Mossad) was
formed in 1937 in collaboration with the Haganah High Command.
Emissaries were dispatched to Germany and Austria to organize
emigration from the European end.

   Jon and David Kimche have written an exciting account of
these daring operations in their book, *The Secret Roads.* The
task of the Mossad emissaries was not necessarily to save Jews
from their tragic plight under Nazi tyranny. "That was not their
job," write the Kimches. "Their eyes were fixes entirely on Palestine
and the British Mandatory. They were looking for young men
and women who wanted to go to Palestine because they wanted
a national home of their own and were prepared to pioneer,
struggle and, if necessary, fight for it. Their interest in those
German Jews who turned to Palestine as a haven of refuge, as
the next best thing after the United States or the United Kingdom,
was secondary to their main purpose."[3]

   The program was consistent with overall Zionist strategy.
It was also, by all accounts, a great success as approximately
80,000 Jews were brought to Palestine by Mossad. Single-minded
purpose, however admirably it is rationalized in terms of results,
can still lead to excesses, which in itself is tragic. Mossad
activities, for example, forced the Palestine Government in
November 1940, to decree that henceforward "illegals" would be

transshipped to a British colony for the duration of the war. Two ships, the *Milos* and the *Pacific*, were then intercepted by a British coast guard patrol and the "illegals" were transferred to the *Patria* for deportation to Mauritius. On November 25 the ship blew up and 202 Jewish immigrants and fifty crew and police lost their lives. "It was an open secret," observe the Kimches, "that it had been organized by the Haganah,"[14] but the legend was accepted that the immigrants had committed suicide to bring attention to the plight of the Jewish refugee and the "injustices" of the mandate immigration policy. "By the organizers of the tragedy and their sympathizers, the story of the *Patria*, twisted out of reality, was seized upon for propaganda which had by now become worldwide, for the blackening of the character of the Palestine administration and the motives of its directors."[15] So writes Albert Hyamson, the onetime director of immigration in Palestine, and a man not unsympathetic to the Jewish National Home. The tragedy had the immediate effect desired. The survivors of the *Patria* were allowed to enter Palestine as legal immigrants.

Criticism has been ceaselessly heaped upon Britain and the Mandate Government for gross insensitivity to the Jewish refugee problem before and during the war. It is, therefore, worth recalling the sober strictures of Albert Hyamson concerning the critics of British policy. Palestine, he points out, was not a rich country, but limited in natural resources and space available for development. In the seven pre-war years of the Hitler regime, Palestine received more than 200,000 Jewish immigrants as compared to only 92,000 in the United States, a country which possessed unparalleled riches and resources. Palestine, in fact, absorbed more immigrants from Axis-dominated Europe than any country in the world.

In 1934 and 1935 the position of German Jews was most precarious owing to their increasing number and viciousness of restrictive laws enacted against them by the Nazis. High Commissioner Sir Arthur Wauchope expressed his hope that the Zionist Organization would allot a large proportion of its labor list to Jews in Germany. The Zionists, however, who had complete control over the selection of immigrants, distributed in 1934 only a quarter of the 14,300 certificates to German Jews. The overwhelming majority of certificates were given to Jews of Eastern Europe, especially to Polish Jews.[6] This discrimination may best be explained by the ethnic origin of Palestinian Jewish leadership which was itself largely Eastern European.

These considerations aside, the gradual pre-war and wartime decimation of European Jewry posed the profoundest moral challenge to the governments of those countries which were spared the horrors of Nazi occupation. It was not just indifference which kept the immigration gates of America, Canada and Britain only partially open to Jewish refugees. Awareness of their plight existed. What was lacking was the decency of simple courage to place human life above political expediency. American Zionists, too, tacitly contributed to this moral failure by not openly attacking the restrictive quota system on immigration. Rather, they saw the quota system itself as proof that theirs was the only viable alternative for the Jews of Europe.

Britain's real dilemma in the tragedy of Palestine was that her realization of the hopeless contradiction which the Mandate involved came too late — much too late. It has been said, not unfairly, that if Herzl was the Marxist theoretician of Zionism, Hitler was the Leninist prime mover of the Jewish State.

Jewish activism followed other courses as well. Raids on British arms' depots increased the supply of illegal weapons available to the Jewish community; at the same time, the Haganah became a major purchaser of contraband war material from all over the world. Activism in an extreme form appeared with groups such as the Irgun and the Stern Gang. These groups, it must be stressed, operated independently of the Jewish Agency and the Zionist leadership during most of the war. The two factions differed at first mainly over who was to be regarded as the chief enemy of Jewish statehood. The Irgun thought it was the Arabs, the Sternists the British.[7]

The Irgun's first venture came in July 1938, when two land mines exploded in the Arab fruit market in Haifa, killing seventy-four and wounding 129. Two Freedom Fighters (as the Sternists were later known) in 1944 assassinated Lord Moyne, the British minister-resident in the Middle East and a member of the war cabinet. Both these acts were denounced by the Jewish Agency, although it is also worth noting that David Ben Gurion did little to check the activities of extremists in the early months of the war. Ben Gurion himself was in direct control of small commando groups which were independent of the Haganah high command. The special squads, or P.O.M., initiated attacks on British property and against at least two Arab villages in the Haifa district.

The extremist societies took firm root from 1944 onward. Ideological differences between the Irgun and the Freedom Fighters gradually vanished as each directed its efforts against the mandate regime. As long as the White Paper remained in force, the Jewish community became increasingly passive toward the efforts, albeit feeble, of British authorities to stamp out the extremists' activities. In fact, the real significance of their program lay in their influence on the uncommitted opinion in the Yishuv.

By the summer of 1945 the war had ended and a new Labor government was installed in Britain. The Laborites had shown strong pro-Zionist sympathies at their annual Blackpool conference. A resolution adopted in the party platform suggested that the Arabs be moved out of Palestine as the Jews moved in. The Jewish community eagerly looked to the government's abandonment of the White Paper and the new foreign secretary, Ernest Bevin, was regarded as the champion of their cause. A dedicated socialist, yet unreservedly British, Bevin was sensitive to the nationalist feelings of people everywhere. However, the stresses of the post-war world, Britain's anxiety over the future of Europe and the looming Soviet threat to Berlin all militated against acting in consonance with his socialist principles. Britain's Asian defense strategy put him at odds with Arab nationalists in the Middle East when he tried to bargain for the renewal of treaties with Egypt and Iraq which granted Britain preferential powers in the maintenance of military bases.

Bevin was forced to swim against the rising tide of Arab nationalism. He argued that a unitary state in Palestine would best serve his country's defense needs. This was not unwelcome to the Palestinians, but Bevin, the optimist, believed that a settlement could be negotiated and he was short tempered with those whom he believed viewed problems with blinkers on their eyes. Arabs were no less obstinate than Zionists in pressing their claims, but he allowed himself to commit disastrous indiscretions when angered by the Zionists' insistence that Palestine was the *only* refuge for European Jewry. Bevin was instantly portrayed as a dyed-in-the-wool anti-Semite. Hard pressed by the American administration, he soon lost control over his policy. The ghost which had bedeviled the entire mandate period returned to haunt Bevin; neutrality between Arab and Jew in Palestine was impossible. Anglo-Zionist relations came to an abrupt end.

Jewish public opinion in Palestine was now more than ever favorably disposed toward terrorism as a means of political pressure. In November 1945, Haganah began negotiations for a merger with the Irgun and the Freedom Fighters. For many months their operations were coordinated under Haganah command which concentrated attacks against British installations and personnel.

Mayhem characterized the declining years of the Mandate. The combined efforts of the Haganah and the terrorists demonstrated a degree of ruthlessness and efficiency which gradually sapped Britain's strength and will to remain in Palestine. Increased illegal immigration, coupled with these military tactics added to the pressure from within.

Meanwhile in the United States, Zionist diplomacy aimed at getting the American Government to exert pressure on Whitehall while whipping up public opinion, both Jewish and non-Jewish, to its banner. In the propaganda war for American and Canadian public opinion Zionists held the trump card. Their great strength was that Zionism could be all things to all men. By contrast the appeal of the Palestinian Arab was simple, and seemed to lack depth and meaning. The Arabs had not asked to be ruled as a British colony, and they wished even less to be subordinated to an alien people. All they had sought was the freedom and independence to determine their own future. The argument was unembroidered and direct. Consequently it left no latitude (unlike Zionism) for subtle appeals to American conscience or prejudice. Zionists, moreover, employed organizational techniques to which the Arabs were wholly unaccustomed. As a result, North American public opinion was uninformed of the real situation, in the sense that it was half-informed, and exposed to only one side of the story. For example, a public opinion poll conducted in Canada in 1946 indicated that there was widespread support for free

Jewish immigration into Palestine although the pollsters noted that this did not necessarily indicate a public commitment to Jewish statehood.

Widely based support in the United States from the local to national level was obtained.[8] Pro-Zionist resolutions were passed in thirty-three State legislatures, by the Congress of Industrial Organizations (C.I.O.) and the American Federation of Labor (A.F. of L.), in both the House of Representatives and the Senate, in the Democratic and Republican Conventions during the presidential campaign of 1944, and again during the congressional elections of 1946. In the White House, President Truman was under the impression that the Zionists were primarily interested in securing a haven for Jewish refugees and that statehood was but a secondary and possible future objective. He therefore advanced the proposal to Prime Minister Attlee of Britain that 100,000 Jews be allowed into Palestine. Attlee reminded the president of promises made to the Arabs, and suggested the creation of a joint Anglo-American Commission which could recommend practical avenues of action on the Palestine question. The commission accepted the Truman proposal, but denied that either Arabs or Jews had the exclusive right to establish a state, recommendations which ensured rejection by both.

The scene of the final diplomatic and political battle for Palestine shifted to the United Nations. Anglo-American cooperation had not provided a solution, and the Zionist war of attrition against Britain forced her to confess the failure of the Mandate and to request the United Nations to place the Palestine question on its agenda. The years of wartime Zionist propaganda were about to pay rich dividends.

An eleven nation Special Committee on Palestine was set up by a General Assembly resolution on May 15, 1947. UNSCOP, as it was known, was confronted with the choice of recommending one of two possible alternatives: either independence in some form, or the continuation of the Mandate. Independence was the course chosen and this meant, in effect, the partition of Palestine into independent Jewish and Arab states. The Zionists had achieved a major victory. The next step was to see that the plan was adopted by the General Assembly.

The Arab position was precarious. The Soviet Union, for

reasons of her own, joined with the United States in backing the partition solution. The Arab states combined could not hope for an outright defeat of the scheme, although there remained the chance that it would not obtain the required thirty-two votes which constituted a two-thirds majority of the Assembly. Amid strenuous efforts on the part of the Arabs and Zionists to secure the precious votes, the U.S. moved in to throw her weight behind the Zionists. The crucial votes were with Haiti, Liberia, Ethiopia, China, the Philippines and Greece. The American Government and allied business interests successfully pressured the home governments of Haiti, Liberia and Ethiopia into altering their original anti-partition vote to one of pro-partition. When the final vote was taken on November 29, 1947, the partition resolution passed by thirty-three votes to thirteen, with ten abstentions. It was a momentous decision, or rather recommendation, for it did not confer any legal privilege. It was at best a compromise, and possibly even the best of compromises, but as Benjamin Disraeli once put it, compromise only ends in catastrophe.

Within the Jewish community of Palestine there was widespread satisfaction over the UN decision, although right-wing political parties were angered at the small size of the proposed Jewish State, which even Ben Gurion described as an "irreducible minimum." The General Assembly had declared that the Jewish State should compromise 56 percent of all Palestine, much less than the Jewish Agency's own partition proposal made in August 1946, but far better than the 1937 Royal Commission scheme. From minority status, owning only 6 percent of the total land area of the country, the Jewish community was gratuitously granted possession of the major part of Palestine with a majority (however slight) over the Arabs living within the area of the proposed Jewish State. The resolution further provided for the total withdrawal of British forces by August 1, 1948, and for a UN Palestine Commission which would supervise the transition period to statehood.

The struggle for a separate State of Israel in the midst of the Arab Middle East now entered the last stage. An undeclared state of war has existed ever since.

8

End of the Mandate

It was obvious to everyone that the resolution could not be implemented without resort to force. The United Nations had no means at its disposal, and none of the major powers was prepared to intervene physically. The decision to use force, therefore, would be made in Palestine, where one side would attempt to enforce the resolution, the other to frustrate it.

In the short weeks between the November resolution and the official end of the Mandate, May 15, 1948, public security in Palestine deteriorated to the vanishing point and essential government services were seriously crippled. The outcome of the impending struggle was by no means a foregone conclusion, but several factors seemed to favor the Jewish community over the Arabs.

First, the Jewish National Home had evolved through provisions in the mandate system into a sub-national government able to operate efficiently and to control all aspects of its community life from public works to military preparation. As the Mandate drew to an end, the Jewish Agency was transformed with comparative ease into the governmental machinery of the Jewish State.

Second, the Zionist leadership enjoyed its recent success in forcing Britain to relinquish responsibility over Palestine, capping this with a political victory in the United Nations. The momentum of the struggle on these fronts flowed over into the struggle against the Arab community. The organic unity of the Jewish community, patterned as it was along European lines, made it relatively easy to conscript and mobilize the entire community for war. The best military personnel of the Haganah, especially the elite corps of the Palmach, were British trained. Moreover, tremendous efforts had been made to buy up stocks of arms of all types which were supplemented by local (illegal) armament factories capable of producing light machine guns and ammunition, grenades, mortar shells, Sten guns, flame throwers, anti-tank guns, and the Davidka heavy mortar. In April 1948, an arms agreement had been negotiated with Czechoslovakia and supplies and weapons began to arrive in Palestine by private airplane and small ships. Heavy armor was brought in after the State of Israel was officially declared.

The Arab community, on the other hand, had suffered the weakening and demoralizing effects of British colonial rule. The Mandatory had made little effort to promote the experience of self-government. When the crisis came the Arabs found they could organize effectively only at the local level. Resistance to partition was patterned after the Arab rebellion, sporadically without any central coordinating machinery whatsoever. But 1948 was different from 1938 in significant ways. The Arab leadership was still forced to work from outside Palestine, although the reconstituted Arab Higher Committee was able to establish some local committees in towns and villages with responsibility for fund raising and the recruitment of a kind of home guard for local defense.

More serious, however, was the general demoralization of the Arab peasantry which was the result of the crushing defeat of the nationalist uprising a decade earlier. During the early months following the end of the war in 1945, the peasants remained passive and quiet, making it doubly difficult for Arab leadership to mobilize them to meet the fresh danger. As a consequence, the burden of the struggle was placed on the shoulders of volunteers who infiltrated from neighboring Arab countries. The "liberate Palestine" movement began in January 1948, but even in March the number of participants did not exceed 5,000; too few to cope with the better trained, better equipped and more numerous Haganah. The Army of Liberation, as the volunteers were called, was only suited to static defensive action. This meant occupying the high ground overlooking some of the major roads, sniping at convoys and disrupting communications. Their main activities were centered on the Tel Aviv-Jerusalem and Jerusalem-Hebron roads, which in fact did not endanger the vast majority of Jewish settlements along the coastal plain and in Galilee. There was little active fighting during the first three months of 1948, although Arabs and Jews alike resorted to the customary but irregular methods of intimidation and retaliation by bomb throwing. Despite spiraling violence on both sides there was no evidence of panic within the Arab community.

The Palestinian leaders of the Arab Higher Committee and the Arab League were playing a wait-and-see political game, hoping that the partition scheme would be reviewed and then abandoned. Even the Americans were already having serious second thoughts about the viability of partition, certain as it was to bring about a violent conclusion to the Mandate. On March 19, 1948, the American delegate to the United Nations proposed the suspension of the partition scheme and that it be replaced with a UN trusteeship. Arab tactics, therefore, seemed justified to a degree, although the failure to prepare an adequate military alternative was, in the long run, disastrous. The Jewish Agency's reaction to the unwelcome developments in the UN was to declare on March 23 that, come what may, a provisional Jewish Government would take over as of May 15. In other words, the UN resolution for partition and statehood would be converted into reality through a simple fait accompli. At the end of March the Haganah high command reached the conclusion that "the only solution is to take the initiative into our own hands, to try to achieve a military decision by going over to the offensive."[11]

Meanwhile, the political committee of the Arab League hesitated, and it was not until the end of April that the decision to intervene in Palestine was made. But by that time it was too late to reverse the course of events which were rapidly consuming the Palestinian Arab community.

With the Haganah decision to go over to the offensive, a plan was devised which completely revised previous defense strategy. Known as Plan D, its objective was "to gain control of the area allotted to the Jewish State and defend its borders, and those blocs of Jewish settlements and such Jewish population as were outside those borders, against a regular or para-regular enemy operating from bases outside or inside the area of the Jewish State."[12] The crucial logistical problem for the Zionists was to replace the de jure authority of Britain (which would end on May 15) with the de facto control of successive areas of the country as they were vacated by British troops. Britain's legal "presence" conveniently provided a shield for these operations against possible attack by the regular Arab armies.

In April 1948 Haganah was in full control of all the Jewish fighting forces, including the Irgun group. Haganah was now responsible for all military operations and the Irgun was obliged to submit its plans to the high command for approval. Both the very influential *Ha'aretz* and the popular *Davar*, the leading lights of the Jewish press in Palestine, voiced their satisfaction at the agreement of cooperation.[3]

On April 1, Haganah commenced the first of thirteen military campaigns under Plan D; eight of these were conducted against Arab villages outside the area allotted to the Jewish State.[4] The primary objective was to carve out a corridor between Tel Aviv and Jerusalem, and to isolate the Holy City. Jewish forces attacked Arab villages, expelling the inhabitants and dynamiting homes so that they could not be re-occupied by the enemy. In a few dramatic days some 10,000 to 15,000 Arabs were launched on the road to refugee camps. Later campaigns conducted in the first two weeks of May were designed to capture the entire northern sector of Galilee. Tiberias, for example, was captured on April 18, and some 5,000 more Arabs joined the growing exodus of villagers. On April 12, an attack by the Irgun against the village of Deir Yassin, which lay to the west of Jerusalem, had tragic consequences for the Arab population. All the inhabitants of the village, 254 men, women and children, were mercilessly murdered and their bodies thrown down a well. The pattern was repeated in the Arab quarter of Jerusalem known as Katamon, on April 29.

At the same time Haganah skillfully employed the subtle weapons of psychological warfare to spread fear and panic thus destroying the will to resist frontal attack by its troops. In one such campaign, leaflets were air-dropped over Galilee signed by the Haganah district commander. He threatened that "all people who do not want this war must leave together with their women and children in order to be safe. This is going to be a cruel war with no mercy or compassion."[5] Haganah was true to its word.

The disasters at Deir Yassin and Katamon were rapidly

magnified many times over as rumors of greater atrocities spread among the population. Peasants were not equipped to cope with this invisible enemy called Fear. As news of the fate of those who had been expelled filtered down through the rural grapevine (aided by more threats over Haganah radio), villagers and peasants took to the roads in fear of their lives taking with them what meager possessions they could carry. Few could have known, or scarcely imagined, that they would never return.

The Arab Higher Committee in the meantime was desperately trying to prevent a mass exodus which it knew would destroy Arab morale and thus hinder the defense of the country. Radio broadcasts and communiqués from the various local committees continually urged the Arabs to remain calm, to stay on the land and in their jobs and homes. Palestinians who had already fled were ordered to return and guard their possessions. Arab volunteers offered stubborn, at times valiant resistance, but were really no match for the Palmach commandos. The tide turned decisively by the third week in April when Haifa and then Jaffa were attacked and occupied by Haganah forces. The fall of Haifa was especially tragic since it was one of the "mixed" towns in which Jews and Arabs had lived side by side in comparative amity.[16]

It was Wednesday, April 21. The British commander had ordered his troops to withdraw to positions outside the city. Haganah received forewarning of the retreat (from the British), and quickly occupied the vacated British posts which were strategically located on the hillside overlooking the Arab quarter of Haifa. Some hours before sunset that day, Haganah began a "psychological blitz" using its radio station and mobile vans to warn the Arabs of the dire consequences of resistance. Promises of safe conduct to Arab territory for all who wanted to leave were broadcast along with the threats. Then machine-gun fire and mortar shells were rained down on the Arab sector where the small 350-man home guard prepared to meet a four-pronged Haganah attack. Gunfire continued throughout the night as the Arab defenders fought to hold onto every building and street corner. The smoke from burning buildings and houses forced the inhabitants into the streets and soon crowds of panic-stricken Arabs were streaming for the safety of the harbor. By noon of the next day several thousand had gathered there while the fighting dragged on.

On Thursday morning an emergency committee of five prominent Arab citizens sought the assistance of the British commander, General Stockwell. The general turned down a request that he intervene with his troops to protect Arab lives and property; he also refused to allow Arab reinforcements to enter the city. The reason for this stand was that Stockwell had been in contact with the Haganah commander from whom he had received the terms for the Arab surrender. These terms were not negotiable. If they were not accepted, Stockwell said that he could not be responsible for further Arab casualties. The Arabs were shocked at this display of partisanship and retired to consider their decision.

By noon Arab resistance had collapsed. Much of the town was in ruins and refugees continued to flee to the harbor where British boats evacuated many of them to Acre. The emergency committee bore the heavy burden of decision, while Stockwell and the Haganah waited for an answer to the terms of surrender. The Jewish mayor, Shabatai Levy, pleaded with the committee not to allow the Arabs to evacuate the city. But Haganah was obviously the party in command and the mayor, for all his genuine sympathy at the plight of the Arabs, could not guarantee their safety. Acceptance of the terms of surrender, therefore, would mean absolving the British of responsibility and conceding to the Haganah's fait accompli, while not ensuring the safety of Arab lives and property. The specter of Deir Yassin still haunted Arab minds. Refusal, on the other hand, would mean the loss of more Arab lives.

Elias Koussa, one of the committee members, still recalls their dilemma: "We thought that the only way out was to ask the general to provide us with eighty trucks daily to transport our properties. We knew well enough that he could not provide this transport, and hoped he would eventually resume control of the town, drive out the Haganah forces from the Arab quarters they had occupied and enable the panicked Arabs crowded in the port area to return home. He did neither and so the flight continued."[7]

Over 50,000 refugees were created by the fall of Haifa. Jaffa was taken a week later and Acre early in May. Both were major towns in the proposed Arab state. Scores of Arab villages in both the Jewish and Arab areas were overrun by Haganah forces. By May 15, the date the Jewish Agency proclaimed the State of Israel, over 250,000 Arabs were homeless, fleeing for refuge wherever they could find it.

Major Edgar O'Ballance has described this phase of the struggle in his book *The Arab-Israeli War: 1948:* "It was the Jewish policy to encourage the Arabs to quit their homes, and they used psychological warfare extensively in urging them to do so. Later, as the war wore on, they ejected those Arabs who clung to their villages. This policy, which had such amazing success, had two distinct advantages. First, it gave the Arab countries a vast refugee problem to cope with, which their elementary economy and administrative machinery were in no way capable of attacking, and secondly, it ensured that the Jews had no fifth column in their midst."[18]

Through the campaigns of Haganah, Ben Gurion's "irreducible minimum" had threatened to become an undefined maximum. The secretary-general of the Arab League cabled the secretary-general of the United Nations on May 15 informing him of the decision of the Arab governments to intervene in Palestine "for the sole purpose of restoring peace and security, and of establishing law and order, and to prevent the spread of disorder and lawlessness into neighboring Arab lands and to fill the vacuum created by the termination of the Mandate."

The first phase of the broadened hostilities was generally in favor of the Arabs, despite the lack of military coordination between the Egyptian movement from the south and the Syrian and Lebanese thrusts from the north. King Abdullah of Transjordan was content to use his well-trained Arab Legion troops mainly for the defense of the area allotted to the Arab State. Until the time of the first cease-fire, which went into effect on June 11, the Arab armies (which were roughly equal in number to the Israeli troops) were unable to "fill the vacuum," a task which had been considered relatively easy to accomplish. But, for the moment at least, further Israeli advances were checked.

The four-week truce period was honored more in the breach than the observance. Both sides took advantage of the lull to regroup and rearm, although the Israelis were able to use the respite to far greater advantage than their opponents. Boatloads of arms reached the coast while tanks and other armored vehicles were airlifted from Czechoslovakia and America. With an eye on the battle ahead, some 30,000 Jewish immigrants were brought into the country and immediately deployed in crucial sectors. When the war entered its second phase the Israelis mustered up to 100,000 troops against the combined total of some 30,000 of the Arab armed force.

The day after the first truce ended on July 9, Israeli forces launched an attack on four fronts. This brilliant campaign, later known as The Ten-Day Offensive, put about 1,000 additional square kilometers of Arab territory under Israeli control: fourteen Arab towns and 200 villages in the area of the Jewish State and 112 villages in the Arab districts were captured and occupied, resulting in the expulsion of tens of thousands more Palestinians. These military successes gave Israel a decisive upper hand in the war. Owing to the ineffective efforts of the United Nations to arrange for a satisfactory settlement, the Israeli leaders were determined to press their advantage and force a military solution of their own on the Arabs.

Ben Gurion, who was now Israel's prime minister and commander in chief of the army, had already declared the partition plan dead and had told a *Time* magazine reporter that the expansion of the "tiny state" of Israel was essential in order to accommodate its future population, which he envisaged might reach ten million people.

A second truce brought The Ten-Day Offensive to an end. It was to prove as impermanent as the first. Using the pretext of Egypt's violation of the cease-fire while refusing permission to United Nations observers to verify the allegations, Israel moved 15,000 of her crack troops into Negev and by the middle of October a large concentration of the Egyptian Army was surrounded at Faluja and cut off from its supply lines. New armed settlements were rushed into the area to bolster the claim of Israeli spokesmen to the whole of the Negev. A similar campaign, preceded by accusations of cease-fire violations, was launched against the remnants of the liberation army in Galilee which was swiftly routed. Another large-scale attack on Egyptian positions carried

Israeli forces right into Sinai and made further resistance impossible. The Egyptian Government decided to enter into armistice negotiations with Israel.

Negotiations commenced in January 1949, on the island of Rhodes under United Nations mediation with a general Egypt-Israeli Armistice Agreement being signed on February 24. An agreement was also concluded with Lebanon toward the end of March. Transjordan consented to negotiations on February 8. Syria followed suit on March 21. Israel, however, still had territorial ambitions against these last two states and hesitated to make an immediate commitment. In particular, Israel sought to obtain an outlet on the Red Sea at Aqaba. Following the collapse of the Egyptian Army, Israeli units began to push south of the Dead Sea where they skirmished with the Arab Legion in December.

Armistice negotiations with Transjordan began on March 4 while Israeli forces continued their southward thrust, finally reaching Aqaba on March 10. The next day Israel signed an "enduring" cease-fire with Transjordan, but still more territory was seized until King Abdullah was forced to invoke his treaty of alliance with Britain. A small contingent of British troops was dispatched to defend Transjordan, but beyond this gesture neither Britain nor the United States was prepared to act. Anxious to avert renewed hostilities, King Abdullah quietly contacted Israeli officials to work out a final settlement. The Israeli bargaining position was strong and their demands simple: Abdullah would cede to Israel some 110 square miles of territory along the central front west of the Jordan which contained several strategic heights of land and much valuable farmland. The king had no choice but to accept and the armistice was signed on April 3. Negotiations with Syria dragged on for a few more weeks as Israel penetrated inside Syrian territory to force her to relinquish portions of Palestine occupied by Syrian troops. An agreement was concluded in July, 1949.

The Mandate had been buried without honor. With the demise of Palestine, Pax Britannica, too, was virtually dead in the Middle

East. Britain not only lost an imperial foothold, but within a decade her prestige and influence vanished as her remaining Arab allies, Abdullah in Jordan, Farouk in Egypt and Nuri in Iraq were removed either by assassination or revolution. In time, however, these wounds would heal. While the post-war revolutionary trends in the Arab world were only in part a backlash of the Palestine War, that conflict itself sprang from the contradictions and antagonisms inherent in the Palestine Mandate. The Palestine War for its part neither resolved the contradictions nor eased the antagonisms.

Israel was the child of British imperialism and Jewish colonialist-nationalism. There need be no embarrassment about using terms which today evoke much emotion and which have become debased through indiscriminate application. Englishmen and Zionists alike were able to plead the virtues of a Jewish national home in Palestine as benefiting British imperial interests; Zionists also regarded themselves as colonists following in the path of the French in North Africa. It is scarcely surprising, therefore, that in an era of decolonization, such as in our present century, the Palestinian Arabs should deeply resent foreign domination under the Mandate and the gradual implantation of a foreign element which threatened to emasculate the Arab identity of their country: a foreign element, which desired, or rather insisted, that it remain distinct and separate from its neighbors.

Palestinians were forced by circumstances to fight for the survival of their community and they lost. Having lost, they were told, in effect, to accept their lot. For the Palestinian however, it was never a question of whether it was nobler "to suffer the slings and arrows of outrageous fortune." Palestinians, then as now, expressed their bewilderment at the Zionists who denied the Arab in principle the very rights they claimed for themselves: "How can the Jew, who has known suffering and torment in his European home, now treat us as others treated him?"

The years drifted by after the war of 1948. The Palestinians tried to accommodate themselves to their new condition, while at the same time never accepting it. One day, perhaps, they would again take up arms against the sea of troubles which had inundated them.

PART TWO

9

The Palestinian Diaspora

The Palestine War marked the beginning of the end for a generation of Arab political leaders who, for three decades, had struggled to win national sovereignty for their people. Freedom from foreign domination was the primary objective in the struggle against the various mandatory and protectorate powers. The nationalist leaders had the wholehearted support of the Arab people and gradually, under nationalist pressure, the symbols of foreign rule were removed. The Tricolor and the Union Jack no longer flew from public buildings in Arab capitals. In their stead the national flags of independent Arab states were proudly unfurled in air which was now freer than before. Alien high commissioners or governors-general no longer ruled in the name of London or Paris. An Arab now spoke for his people.

All this the Old Order had accomplished. Yet, as the Arab political elite took control of the governments of their countries, the relationship between them and their people underwent change. Various symbols of foreign rule remained and Arabs were aware that their independence was a highly qualified one. The Old Order had purchased independence at the price of treaty arrangements with their former overlords. Britain's Mandate over Iraq ended in 1930, but her position was only modified by a treaty which was to last for twenty-five years and which gave Britain important rights in Iraq's military affairs and foreign policy. Anglo-Egyptian relations were reorganized in 1936 along the same lines. Military bases were maintained in both countries and foreign troops stationed on theoretically independent national soil. Although the last French soldier left Lebanon and Syria in 1946, France retained a privileged status in both countries.

Troops and treaties were viewed by many Arabs as inconsistent with their formal independence. The "mutual assistance" clauses in the treaties were ludicrous enough if one could imagine Iraqi soldiers rushing to the defense of Britain under attack from some third power. The situation appeared quite sinister, on the other hand, if British troops were used in Iraq to spare that country some unspeakable peril known only to the "inner circle" of the cabinet in Whitehall and of absolute irrelevance to anyone in Iraq. Nevertheless, in the name of the Anglo-Iraqi treaty, British forces marched into Baghdad in May 1941, and overthrew the government of Rashid Ali. In February of the following year the British ambassador in Cairo ordered British troops to surround the palace of King Farouk to impress upon His Majesty the choice of leaving the country or of installing a prime minister acceptable to Britain. Even the reactionary and corrupt Farouk could not have devised a better plan to create for himself the image of a martyr to foreign oppression. (Such perhaps is the nature of all mutual assistance agreements, as the Czechs found to their sorrow in the summer of 1968 when Warsaw Pact troops were dispatched to Prague to save the Czechs from themselves. Which party is mutual assistance supposed to assist if not the strongest member of the alliance?)

Unnoticed and unheeded, a younger generation of Arabs had emerged during this first nationalist phase. Many had been educated abroad in the quiet, cloistered colleges of Oxford and Cambridge or in the intellectual beehive of the Sorbonne in cosmopolitan Paris. Others took whatever roads were available for advancement and consequently the lower ranks of the officer corps of the army attracted young men of the new middle class. Their attitude indicated the growing generation gap — an abyss — between them and the Old Order politicians who came under attack for abandoning the Arab mission once independence had been attained. The Old Order had satisfied the national emotion for independence, but the earlier memory of betrayal by Britain and France after World War I soon faded. Close ties with the former rulers suited well the vested interests representing the feudal, commercial and industrial elements of society. These same nationalists were now being held responsible by their younger, angry and erstwhile supporters for continuing social and economic difficulties, and for the failure to gain more complete concessions from the European powers. The material needs of the people also had to be met. The fight against social inequality, poverty and illiteracy was scarcely begun.

The Palestine War of 1948 brought matters to a head. The old civilian and military leaderships were thoroughly discredited and were not equipped to meet the new challenge. The younger generation, however, did not have the political power to effect the changes which the times required.

During that fateful war, a young Egyptian army major sat among his men at Faluja in Palestine. They were surrounded by Israeli troops. Shells fell about them and enemy aircraft buzzed overhead. Food and medical supplies were inadequate and their weapons outdated and worthless. The young major thought to himself: "Here we are in these foxholes, surrounded, and thrust treacherously into a battle for which we are not ready, our lives the playthings of greed, conspiracy and lust which have left us here weaponless under fire." They had fought courageously but were demoralized by the corruption of their own leaders. A brigadier, who was a known trafficker in narcotics, had made a fortune recovering weapons abandoned in the western desert after World War II which he then sold to the Egyptian Government. Rumor had it that King Farouk shared in the profits of this deal.

Four years later, on a particularly humid July night, this same young officer led a group of his colleagues in the officers corps in a coup which overthrew the ruling oligarchy and sent the king into exile. This was Gamal Abdel Nasser, a man destined by humiliating defeat to become a decisive force in contemporary Arab history. The figurehead of the coup, General Muhammad Neguib, summed up the motivation of the Free Officers: "To serve its purpose, the military must be given a worthy government to defend; if the government is manifestly indefensible then the military must either resign itself to the prevailing corruption or intervene in civil affairs."

It is against this background that the intrusion of the military into politics can be understood, not only in Egypt, but also in Syria and later in Iraq.

For others, the Palestine War contained its own bitter lesson. Musa Alami was a Cambridge-educated lawyer who had served as Crown Counsel in the Palestine Government for several years, and in 1945 he sat as representative of Palestine on the Committee of Foreign Ministers which drew up the constitution of the Arab League. To Musa the Arab defeat was a two-edged sword. In Palestine itself, defeat stemmed from the Arabs' fundamental weakness: their lack of preparation, their lack of unity and their lack of arms.

"We proceeded along the lines of previous revolutions while the Jews proceeded along the lines of total war... it was obvious that our aims in the battle were diverse; the aim of the Jews was solely to win."

How did all this come about? Alami's answer is multi-fold. Palestine reflected the condition of the Arab world in general. Disunity on the battlefield was the result of political and military shortcomings and the lethargy of Arab governments, stemming from the absence of popular control because the Arab peoples themselves were weak. While his analysis was critical and frank, he did not underestimate the danger of Israel to the whole Arab nation: "The ambitions of the Jews are not limited to Palestine alone but embrace other parts of the Arab world... the next step will be an attempt to take all of Palestine and then they will proceed according to circumstances — circumstances which they themselves will attempt to create."[11]

As early as 1919 the Zionists had sought at the Paris Peace Conference what they regarded as the minimum territorial requirements of the Jewish National Home. For reasons of economic and defensive viability the Home should include what today is southern Lebanon up to the Litani River, large portions of fertile southern Syria and Transjordan, and an unspecified part of the Sinai peninsula. Israel was still an undefined quantity but Alami and many Arab intellectuals believed in 1948 that, given the chance, Israel would expand: the weakness of the Arab peoples would lead to that temptation.

Musa Alami would have understood Ben Gurion's sentiment when he said that "nowadays wars are not fought just by armies, but rather the whole nation must be mobilized." The Arab nation was no exception. The prescription for weakness was unity and the mobilization of the entire Arab people.

Arab unity or Pan-Arabism has dominated popular political sentiment since World War II. The idea had been the undercurrent of nationalist thinking since World War I, but the Arab-Israeli War lent a sense of urgency for concrete results. The intention of all Arab nationalists was to liberate, unite, revive and reconstruct the Arab world. Their mission was to conduct a campaign against western influence and domination, to build the Arab nation and to adopt revolutionary action against intellectual, moral, social, political and economic evils. Arab Unity is therefore a powerful psychological force and in this sense a political reality and a source of social ferment.

Liberation from British inflence and control was achieved by stages as the treaty system dissolved with accompanying violence, as in Egypt 1954-56, and in Iraq in 1958. After seven bitter years of guerilla warfare the Algerians finally drove out the French, and Algeria became independent in 1962. As colonialism beat its bloody retreat from the desert sands, the United States, haunted by paranoid visions of communism, rushed in to fill the void with guns and pledges gift-wrapped and tied with strings which led straight back to the Pentagon. Arabs generally were unimpressed by the mutual rantings of the two cold war giants, Russia and the United States, and they had no desire to be caught in the web of an ideological struggle which did not concern them.

Besides, the Arabs were preoccupied with their own cold war. Since 1948, the Arab world had been deeply divided and the force of Pan-Arabism greatly dissipated whenever the theme of unity was advocated by different leaders representing different interests.

The Suez crisis of 1956 demonstrated President Nasser's uncanny capacities as a tactician, turning the political tables on his French, British and Israeli adversaries. The union of Syria and Egypt into the United Arab Republic two years later made him the unchallenged leader of the Arab revolutionary movement, but not for long.

In 1958 General Abdul Karim Qasim overthrew the decrepit pro-western regime of Nuri Said in Iraq, and initiated a widely

popular program of reform. Qasim became a challenger to Nasser's
title of revolutionary leader of the Arabs. Their regimes were
at loggerheads and a split in the Arab "left" swiftly developed.
Syria pulled out of the United Arab Republic in 1961. Qasim
was eliminated in 1963, after which the central issue of Arab
leadership was a struggle between the "revolutionaries" led by
Nasser and the "reactionaries" who had no acknowledged leader.
This latter group includes the monarchical regimes of Jordan,
Saudi Arabia. Morocco and until 1969, Libya when its aged ruler
was deposed in an army coup. The lines between the two warring
camps were not, however, always clearly drawn because it was
possible (albeit embarrassing) for President Nasser and King
Faysal of Saudi Arabia to try and compose their differences over
the Republican-Royalist civil war in Yemen.

All these examples of disunity within the Arab family provoked
many observers of the Middle East scene to say cynically that
nothing unites the Arab states except their collective hatred of
Israel, an observation which has become part of the rich western
treasury of myths about the Arab world. Professor Malcolm
Kerr's more perceptive analysis is that "when the Arabs are in a
mood to cooperate, this tends to find expression in an agreement
to avoid action on Palestine, but when they choose to quarrel,
Palestine policy readily becomes a subject of dispute. The prospect
that one Arab government may unilaterally provoke hostilities with
Israel arouses fears among others for their own security, or at
least for their political reputation."[2]

The accuracy of this analysis is reflected in the theory which
was current from the late nineteen-fifties that the Palestine Problem
could not be resolved before the fulfillment of the revolution in
each Arab country. The economic, social and political transformation
of the Arab community, in other words, must precede direct
action on the question of Palestine. The focus logically shifted
away from Israel and onto the Arab community itself, although
this theory was as much a rationalization of the recognized
weaknesses in Arab society as it was sound revolutionary strategy.
Nevertheless, the decade following the Suez crisis marked a period
of rapid economic growth and social change among Israel's
neighbors, together with the first abortive attempts at political
unity.

However, in certain government circles, and among the Arab intelligentsia generally, a deep dilemma had to be faced. The Arab Revolution was committed not only to progress and development but also to the eradication of colonialism from every portion of its national soil. Israel was a *fait colonial*, the creation of which had resulted in the destruction of Palestinian society and the displacement of hundreds of thousands of Arabs from their homes and lands. The Palestinian became to the Arab what the Jew in Europe was to the Christian, a burden of guilt on his conscience. And Palestinians, bereaved of their land, would not permit the burden to be eased.

As a political entity Palestine had disappeared from the map, but the idea survived in the minds and hearts of a people sentenced to exile; an idea, moreover, which is deeply rooted in the land. A poet writes: "In the briar-covered mountains I saw you, a shepherdess without sheep, pursued among the ruins." The shepherdess is the poet's lover, Palestine personified, but without her flock, her own people. The symbol is a simple and honest one which time can neither tarnish nor eradicate.

As well as a *fait colonial*, Israel was a *fait accompli*, with powerful financial and diplomatic support in every major country of the Western world, especially the United States which, after World War II, replaced Britain as the center of Zionist pressure. The western commitment to Israel, like earlier British support for the Jewish National Home, involved the same set of contradictions which had long been inherent components of the conflict. Support for the Jewish State naturally implies acceptance of the historical context out of which the state was born and the ideological foundations upon which it is based.

Statistics reveal the magnitude of the catastrophe which befell the Palestinian community but they do not measure the full enormity of the disaster. Over 750,000 refugees were created by the Palestine War. A third of this number had already fled before the State of Israel was proclaimed in mid-May of 1948. After the first truce Israeli forces drove more than 60,000 Arabs from the Lydda-Ramleh area with little more than the possessions they could carry with them. During the second truce which followed The Ten-Day Offensive tens of thousands of Arabs were sent into exile from the Negev and Galilee before the advancing Israeli Army. As late as the fall of 1950, one year after the armistice agreements, some 7,000 Bedouin tribesmen were expelled from Israel and more Arabs were driven from the Israel-Syrian demilitarized zone in the summer of 1951.

By 1966, the number of refugees had rocketed to almost 1.4 million owing to a very high birthrate. The refugees were scattered in their pathetic hordes throughout the neighboring Arab countries. In 1948 the figures were 280,000 in Arab Palestine, 70,000 in Transjordan, 100,000 in Lebanon, 75,000 in Syria, 190,000 in Gaza, 7,000 in Egypt and 4,000 in Iraq. When King Abdullah of Transjordan annexed Arab Palestine to his kingdom in December 1948, he acquired the Arab refugees from Israeli-occupied Palestine, that is, the State of Israel. By 1950 when the United Nations Relief and Works Agency assumed responsibility for the refugees, about 30 percent of the total were living in sixty organized camps while the remaining 70 percent were scattered in the towns and villages of the host countries.

The other dimension of this exodus of Arabs from their homes and lands was the vast wealth of property they left behind. Some 80 percent of Israel's total land area was land abandoned by the Arab refugees. This abandoned property was one of the greatest contributions toward making Israel a viable state. For example, 350 of the 370 new Jewish settlements established in the five years after independence were on absentee Arab property; 10,000 shops and businesses of all description were left in Israeli hands; half of Israel's citrus groves were on Arab property and in 1951 Arab fruit provided 10 percent of Israel's foreign currency earnings; the olive crop from Arab-owned lands provided Israel's third largest export. A conservative estimate of the total value of abandoned movable property and land came to over 120 million Palestinian pounds, or $336 million.

In 1948 the dimensions of the Palestine Problem suddenly seemed infinite. Humanitarian, economic, political and social questions were all closely linked and progress on one aspect could be impeded by stalemate on another.

The most immediate task was to spare the refugees from the indiscriminate sickle of the Grim Reaper. Without adequate medical supplies, sustenance and shelter, the oncoming winter months, which in the Middle East can be harsh by any standards, threatened to decimate the refugee population. Through the summer of 1948 the Arab governments provided for the Palestinians to the extent their own meager resources would allow. The situation required more drastic measures. Largely as a result of the initiative of the United Nations mediator, Count Folke Bernadotte, interim emergency aid was secured from some European countries and from private relief agencies. The United Nations moved in officially to provide aid through various of its specialized agencies until the UN Relief and Works Agency was established. Nevertheless, refugee relief was regarded as a merely temporary expedient which a formal peace settlement would render unnecessary.

It was of course impossible to wipe out overnight the causes of the conflict which extended back over the preceding half century.

To the international community, to the world at large looking at the Middle East, the question of refugees is primarily a humanitarian problem. To the Arabs, on the other hand, and above all to the Palestinians themselves, the basic configuration is political. The Arab Higher Committee, backed by the Arab League, proclaimed an All-Palestine Government in September 1948, to be centered in Gaza. Its elected president was Hajj Amin Husseini. At a national congress, convened on October 1 in Gaza, it was resolved that "on the basis of the natural and historical rights of the Arab people of Palestine to freedom and independence... we proclaim the establishment of a free and democratic state, working for the realization of the freedom and rights of the people."[3]

It was a hollow proclamation when the so-called Palestinian State was half-occupied by the State of Israel which had been recognized by the two super-powers, Russia and the United States. The Government of Gaza, cut off as it was from the rest of Palestine, made little sense. Moreover, Hajj Amin's political fortunes were spent. The disaster of the Palestine War left him with no credit or credibility and he departed from the scene to become the most widely maligned and villified of the Palestinian leaders. Despite the immediate material needs of the vast majority of its people, the All-Palestine Government nevertheless gave notice that the struggle for the realization of the freedom and rights of the Palestinian people had not been abandoned.

More significant was the move by King Abdullah of Transjordan to annex the remnant of Palestine to his kingdom. Abdullah had been installed as the Prince of Transjordan by the British after World War I. The gesture was supposed to fulfill British promises made to Abdullah's father, King Hussein of the Hijaz, for Arab "independence" as set forth in the McMahon-Hussein correspondence. The desert kingdom was, in any case, an administrative unit under the Palestine Mandate with a special British resident designated to handle all of Abdullah's affairs. When the United Nations resolution recommended the partition of Palestine in November 1947, Abdullah was quick to see the material advantage of adding the proposed Arab State to Transjordan. He initiated secret negotiations with the Zionists as early as November 1947.[4]

His first contacts were with Mrs. Golda Meyerson who, twenty-one years later, as Mrs. Golda Meir, would become Israel's fourth prime minister. Abdullah was anxious to come to an understanding with the Jews and avoid, if possible, a war over Palestine. That nothing materialized was due in part to the strong line adopted by the Arab League, which Abdullah could not openly oppose, and in part by the total lack of Zionist concessions which might have strengthened the king's hand. Even after war had broken out Abdullah was interested in a formal peace with the provisional Government of Israel. Negotiations revealed, however, that Israel was using its military advantage to extract the greatest possible concessions from Abdullah. (Colonel Moshe Dayan was the chief Israeli negotiator in the second round of talks.) Negotiations dragged on in secret for several months until the news leaked out, and Palestinian reaction made a settlement virtually impossible.

King Abdullah made more headway with the Palestinians in implementing his scheme. The shock waves of defeat and humiliation rippled through the whole Palestine community. Palestinian leadership had crumbled and the Arab armies were incapable of pursuing the war to a successful conclusion. The Palestinians needed some form of stable and secure regime and Abdullah offered this with his plan of annexation. The Gaza

Congress, however, appeared as a challenge to his authority. Leaving nothing to chance, Abdullah convened his own Palestine Congress in Amman which denounced the Gaza Government and petitioned the king to place Arab Palestine under his protection. In response to this "request," Abdullah called together a second meeting at Jericho on December 1, 1948, at which time he was proclaimed king of all Palestine. The resolutions of the congress were ratified by the Jordanian Parliament two weeks later and the annexation was formally complete. Annexation evoked loud cries of protest from other Arab governments; Abdullah was accused of trying to liquidate the Palestine Problem, which was in fact the case. The Palestinian delegates to the congress, on the other hand, took the long-term view that the union would not affect their ultimate objective of restoring to Palestinians the rights to their land. The first resolution of the Jericho meeting expressed thanks for the efforts and sacrifices of the Arab governments, and requested their continued support in the fight to save Palestine. Another resolution urged the need for haste in helping the refugees to return to their country.

Palestinians as a whole were encouraged to hope that their rights could be achieved since these rights had been internationally acknowledged. On December 11, 1948, the General Assembly of the United Nations passed a resolution to that effect. Paragraph eleven noted that "refugees wishing to return to their homes and live in peace with their neighbors should be permitted to do so at the earliest practicable date, and that compensation should be paid for the property of those choosing not to return, and for the loss or damage to property..."

Earlier Count Bernadotte, the United Nations mediator, had reported that no settlement could be just or complete if recognition were not accorded to the rights of the Arab refugee to return to the home from which he had been dislodged by the hazards and strategy of the armed conflict. From the beginning, therefore, the principle of the right of return has been for the Palestinians the sine qua non of any settlement. The annual reiteration of this principle in United Nations resolutions has helped keep alive this hope.

Time has, if anything, deepened and intensified the Palestinian refugees' longing to return. Apart from dispensing relief, UNRWA has made repeated efforts to initiate works projects and development programs to help integrate refugees into the economic life of the area on a self-sustaining basis, all in the hope that in this way both the political and practical aspects of the refugee problem might be solved through economic means. The Arab governments were at first extremely reluctant to support the refugees' economic integration, fearing that this would prejudice their right of repatriation to Israel.

There were other practical difficulties as well. First, the host countries, with the exception of Syria, were poor in natural resources and already overpopulated. For example, the influx of refugees into Lebanon increased its population by 10 percent. Jordan alone supported more than half the total number of refugees. It would be difficult for the Arab governments to make fiscal sacrifices on the scale required to integrate the Palestinians, for this would entail holding back on development programs planned for the benefit of their own citizens. In addition, even the largest of the proposed UNRWA works projects would only absorb some 200,000 refugees, a figure slightly greater than the anticipated increase in the refugee population at the time of the projects' completion.

Second, the vast majority of the refugees, or roughly 80 percent of the total, were either farmers or unskilled workers who would have to compete in a market already saturated with farmers and laborers. The more fortunate minority was able to integrate easily and UNRWA provided educational facilities and opportunities for others.

The third, and perhaps most significant factor hindering Palestinian reintegration, was the attitude of the refugees themselves. Henry Labouisse, the then director of UNRWA, reported in February 1957, that the situation was almost unchanged owing to the political aspect of the problem and to deep-seated human emotions. The reason, he said, did not "lie simply in the field of economics. UNRWA can, to be sure, enable some hundreds of refugees to become self-supporting each year — through small agricultural development projects, grants to establish small businesses and the like. But it cannot overcome the fact that the refugees as a whole insist upon the choice provided for them in the General Assembly resolution (December 11, 1948), that is, repatriation or compensation. In the absence of that choice, they bitterly oppose anything which has even the semblance of a permanent settlement elsewhere."

In 1963 I was taken through one of the largest camps in Jordan by a Palestinian friend. This was Jericho, lying near the River Jordan just north of the Dead Sea. Jericho goes back in human memory to the third millenium before Christ and is the place where Joshua fought his bloodiest battle. After 1948 and up to the outbreak of the Six Day War, this ancient spot contained a refugee camp of over 70,000 souls. Today it is desolate and deserted, its inhabitants joining after the war the tens of thousands of new refugees on the east bank of the Jordan.

A minor crisis had seized the camp when we arrived. UNRWA officials were trying to persuade the camp council to permit the whitewashing of the mud huts of their shantytown. If anything could cheer up these one-roomed hovels a fresh daub of white might do it. The council, however, politely declined permission because they feared that any real improvement in their situation would merely add a degree of permanency to their exile. At the time I was shocked at the apparent callousness of the council's position; later, when I had talked with other Palestinians in other camps in Jordan and Lebanon, I began to realize the depth of their sentiment for their former homes and lands. Children who had been born in the camps talked of "home" as though they knew every inch of ground, every tree and bush.

Walid, my companion, was just sixteen years old. He had been born a year before the Palestine War. His father was a schoolteacher in Tulkarm which was located on the armistice line on a height of land overlooking the fertile plain which had fallen to Israel. Walid was fortunate in that his father could provide his brothers and sisters with a normal home life; he had never lived in the camps, although he knew them well. His life had been more complete than the listless monotonous existence of camp life. Nevertheless, he spoke as passionately as his refugee brother about returning, but for another reason. From the roof of his house in Tulkarm, Walid pointed out to me the fields below cultivated by Israeli farmers: "You see that piece of land there, beyond the railway tracks and to the right of that house?

My grandfather owned that house and the land around it. It is good land, is it not? Someday..."

I had heard it all before. We walked down the main street of the town past the cinema and toward the "frontier." A single iron post marked the boundary line. Walid laughed and said: "We play a game with the Israelis." He pulled the stake out of the ground, carried it a few paces forward and drove it into the ground. "Tomorrow, someone from over there will move it back, and then one of us will shift it again." I wondered if their game constituted a violation of the armistice agreements! The Israeli-Jordanian armistice lines in several places had deprived Arab villagers of access to their lands, or had divided Arab towns and villages into two sectors. It was this factor which originally contributed to the high level of "infiltration" into Israeli-held territory after the conclusion of the war.

It was near Jericho that Musa Alami founded his Arab Development Society. Shortly after the war of 1948, Musa and a handful of refugees began their search for underground sources of fresh water in the wasteland of Judea where the experts all agreed that water did not exist. But water was found and slowly, arduously, they began to reclaim the barren land and make it thrive. From their intensive labors a fertile oasis gradually emerged until some 2,000 acres supported refugees in a variety of agricultural enterprises. Refugee orphans are also given vocational training in a special school in this unique Palestinian village.

It is strange to westerners that Musa Alami's triumph did not lessen the desire of the village's inhabitants to see the Palestinian community restored. A later commissioner-general of UNRWA, John Davis, stated in his Annual Report for 1964 that the Palestinians did not see themselves as consciously breaking with their past in order to seek a new life in new surroundings. "The Palestine refugees," he said, "regard themselves, rather, as temporary wards of the international community whom they hold responsible for the upheaval which resulted in their having to leave their homes. As they see it, the international community has a duty to enable them to return to their homes and, meanwhile, to provide for their maintenance and welfare."

Such are the factors hindering the process of Palestinian

integration into the surrounding Arab environment. Other equally
important factors have contributed to preventing the repatriation
of the exiled Palestinians, thereby prolonging the conflict to the
present day. These factors relate to the Israeli perspective of
the Palestine Problem.

Under the Mandate for Palestine, the Jewish Agency had
never at any time formulated a positive policy of cooperation
with the Arab population. Indeed, implicit in Zionist ideology and
explicit in practice, the Arabs were excluded from consideration
in the functions of the Jewish National Home. Separate development of the Arab and Jewish communities was the rule. Any
other arrangement would, in the Zionist view, impair the
specifically Jewish character or personality of the National Home.

Palestinians had perceived that in the absence of political
power in the hands of their community, the Mandate would be
used to change the demographic character of Palestine *as a whole,*
and that ultimately, through the mechanics of the imposed
Mandate, an alien European (and Jewish) community would
assume political control over their land. Thus, from the very
beginning, Palestinians demanded representative democratic
institutions as the first step to independence, while Zionists
insisted that the question of independence be held in abeyance
until a Jewish majority was achieved. As a result of war and the
Arab exodus, Zionists were left in control of an area 22 percent
larger than the partition scheme (they now held 70 percent
of the whole of Palestine) with a negligible Arab minority, since
only about 150,000 Palestinians remained in what became the
State of Israel.

10

The Peace that didn't Come

The Palestinians were now on the outside, determined in the long run to get back in. The Israelis were equally determined to keep them out. But whereas Israel's military victory had been decisive, there remained the political task of searching for principles on which peace might be based. From a position of military superiority, the young Israeli Government insisted upon direct negotiations with the various Arab governments. It was felt that this would lessen the chances of outside pressures forcing her to make concessions detrimental to her national interests. And above all, Israel's national interests demanded *security*. That was a purely practical necessity, although it gave, in effect, a lower priority to *peace*. The general Israeli attitude was: "We needn't run after peace; peace will come when the Arabs are resigned to our reality." Today, after twenty years, Israel's argument for peace, based on the theory of attrition, has proven as dangerously sterile as the attitude of Arab leaders who have held that if Israel is ignored altogether it would conveniently disappear.

Ironically, after 1948 Israelis found themselves in the same position vis-à-vis the Arab states as the Palestinians had been vis-à-vis the Zionists during the Mandate. It now appeared to the Israelis that the Arabs only wanted to negotiate the details of the emasculation of the Jewish identity of Israel by insisting on the Palestinians' right of return. The Zionist objective of a Jewish state had been achieved. It was not about to be jeopardized by receiving a fifth column of Palestinian refugees within its frontiers. The force of circumstances and the memory of past experience were now more compelling than the will to move decisively toward peace.

However, expediency alone did not determine the framework of Israeli national interests. As an Israeli Government pamphlet entitled *Facts and Figures*, published in 1955, notes: "the State of Israel does not exist for its own sake but as the instrument for the implementation of the Zionist ideal." Since its inception in Basle, Switzerland, seventy-two years ago, the Zionist ideal has been the promotion of a solution to the problem of anti-Semitism by conferring national status on the Jewish people, which could then re-create its national life within the historic frontiers of Palestine. It is this ideological component of Zionism which has caused Palestinians to fear that the consummation of Zionism is not the State of Israel as established in 1948.

After statehood was attained, Prime Minister Ben Gurion spelled out Israel's continuing mission. In the Introduction to the 1951-1952 *Israel Government Yearbook* Ben Gurion observes that "the cardinal aim of our State is the redemption of the people of Israel, the ingathering of the exiles." For this purpose the organic link between the World Zionist Organization and the Government of the State of Israel was formalized by a status law for the world body in 1952. The W.Z.O. was charged with responsibility for immigration and settlement policy — a unique arrangement whereby a sovereign government delegates such a function to a non-governmental, ideological body. Ben Gurion continued: "A primary and deciding factor in our security is mass immigration in swift tempo." Immigration from the Jewish Diaspora to Israel is therefore defined both in terms of the national interest (security) and of ideology (liquidation of the Diaspora).

Concerning Zionist territorial objectives, Ben Gurion is equally candid. In the 1952-53 *Yearbook* he stated it "must now be said that the State of Israel has been established in only a portion of the Land of Israel." The 1955-56 *Yearbook* reiterates this position: "The creation of the new State by no means derogates from the scope of historic Eretz Israel." A similar theme was echoed with more practical effect by Israeli officials at the time of the Israeli invasion of Egypt in 1956. On the morning of the attack, Walter Eytan, then director general of the Ministry of Foreign Affairs, broadcast that "Israel is not out to wage war or conquer territory; her aim is to defend her security and the lives of her people against the attacks of Egyptian guerilla forces."[1] A week later, in the Knesset, Prime Minister Ben Gurion said "our forces did not infringe upon the territory of the land of Egypt and did not even attempt to do so... Our operations were restricted to the area of the Sinai Peninsula."[2] He spoke of "freeing" Sinai and "liberating" a part of the ancient homeland. These irredentist hopes were quashed at the time by strong pressure from the U.S. Government which reacted in cold fury to the tri-partite invasion of Egypt.

While it is true that there is neither a Zionist nor Israeli concensus on the territorial question, to the Arabs there is little doubt that the campaigns for *aliya* (Jewish immigration) imply a policy of expansion. Immediately after the Six Day War in June 1967, with Israeli troops in occupation of Gaza and Jordan's West Bank (the remainder of the former mandated territory of Palestine), a serious debate was joined in Israel on the question of *aliya* in the altered circumstances created by the war. The subject was widely discussed in the Israeli press. The late Prime Minister Levi Eshkol himself referred to the urgent importance of increased immigration as a "pillar of Israel's security."[3] Already parts of the occupied territories (especially the Golan Heights in Syria) have been removed from the bargaining block as new Jewish settlements have been established.

Statehood, from the beginning of Zionist ideology had become smoothly assimilated to the Israeli national interest. Israel's foreign policy was based on the need to preserve the territorial and ethnic integrity of the State, a need which was rationalized in terms of the security policy.

Ideological and pragmatic considerations were evident in Israel's resistance to the early attempts to repatriate the Palestinian refugees. During the first truce period in the '48 war, and before the last major Israeli offensive, Ben Gurion told his cabinet that none of the refugees should be allowed to return. Influential sections of the Hebrew press supported him and all the leading newspapers placed the blame for the Palestinians' flight on the Arab governments and Britain.[4] *Ha-Boqer*, the daily of the General Zionist faction contrived a justification for rejecting repatriation which struck a discordant note with previous propaganda appeals. Israel, it argued, suffered from an unfavorable land population ratio, possessing only 1/100 of the land area of the Middle East and yet 1/60 of its population; nevertheless, Israel was prepared to accept hundreds of thousands of Jewish refugees while the Arab countries with their vast territories were unwilling to integrate their fellow Arabs.[5]

In contrast, one of the prominent themes of Zionist propaganda in the nineteen-twenties and thirties had been that Palestine was sufficiently under-developed and under-populated to support as many as three or four million new Jewish settlers. Suddenly in 1948 the land was too small and congested to welcome back its indigenous inhabitants.

The maximum concession Israel was prepared to make was a partial repatriation of 100,000 refugees on condition that the territorial status quo and the principle of the non-return of the majority of Palestinians were accepted by the Arab governments. Not only the Arabs, but the United Nations and the U.S. Government found the proposal inadequate. Israeli public opinion was also aroused — but not because of its shortcomings; rather because it conceded too much. Foreign Minister Moshe Sharett came under fire from the members of his own party. A commonly heard rebuke of his policy was that the return of any number of Arabs would deprive future Jewish settlers of land.

In June 1949, Ben Gurion replied to a note from President Truman in which the president had described Israel's attitude as a threat to peace. The prime minister repeated his government's position concerning the security risk involved in allowing Arabs to return and he added that on humanitarian grounds alone it would be better to resettle the Palestinians elsewhere, since their homes had been either destroyed or occupied by Jewish immigrants.

Ben Gurion had not exaggerated — Jewish immigrants now poured into Israel. During its first three and a half years the young state absorbed nearly 700,000 new settlers. Israel's population soared by 108 percent. This was indeed "mass immigration in swift tempo." New social and legal realities were rapidly being created in Israel, a kind of non-military fait accompli which could be used to buttress the argument for the non-return of refugees.

On June 24, 1948, the Abandoned Areas Ordinance was

issued by the Israeli Government. Under the Ordinance, a custodian of abandoned (or absentee) property was appointed who, on the strength of his own personal judgment could declare any movable or immovable Arab property in Israel "abandoned." This was the first of a series of laws and regulations designed to bring a chaotic situation under control and to create more land for Jewish settlers by expropriation and confiscation of Arab land and property.

On December 12, 1948, the Absentee Property Regulations were passed and the legal relationship between the Arabs and their property defined. Professor Peretz notes that the regulations in effect "prevented the return of any Arab, including those who were citizens of Israel, to property abandoned during, or immediately before, the war."[16] The definition of an absentee was made so inclusive that a Palestinian who had happened to visit Beirut, or even Nablus or Tulkarm, for a single day during a period covering the last six months of the Mandate up to September 1, 1948, automatically forfeited his rights to his property under Israeli law. These regulations created 30,000 "refugees" in Israel itself, persons who had never left the country but who had gone from their own town or village to another nearby in the course of the hostilities. By the end of 1948 and before the armistice negotiations had begun, the question of the return of Arab refugees to their lands and properties was, in the eyes of the Israeli lawmakers, a purely academic concern. Not only was repatriation impractical, it was now legally impossible. Although there was justification for the Israeli insistence that all outstanding problems including the refugees be treated within the framework of an overall peace settlement, Israeli domestic policy virtually precluded any settlement based on United Nations resolutions.

Later, Israel officially abandoned the repatriation issue altogether. The only feasible solution was the resettlement of the Palestinians in Arab countries. Israel's representative to the United Nations, Abba Eban (presently his country's foreign minister), argued the case before the General Assembly in November 1958. With his customary eloquence (he has been called The Voice of Israel) Eban said that "the refugees are all Arabs; and the countries in which they find themselves are Arab countries. Yet the advocates of repatriation contend that these Arab refugees should be settled in a non-Arab country, in the only social and cultural environment which is alien to their background and tradition."[17] Repatriation would mean "uprooting" the refugee from his camp and "alienating" him from Arab society. The ideological basis of the argument is clear. From the Israeli perspective, the Palestinians as a people are denied any share in the land of their fathers. Recalling the early days, Prime Minister Golda Meir has remarked that when the Jews came to Palestine after World War I there was no such thing as Palestinians. "It was not as though there was a Palestinian people and we came and threw them out and took their country away from them. They did not exist."[18] (And Abba Eban has also claimed that the Palestinians have no role in any future peace settlement.)[19] While the security argument, and its later more sophisticated versions were used consistently and vigorously to prevent the repatriation of the Palestinian refugees, the same argument was employed in relation to the Arab minority which had remained in Israel after the '48 war.

As much as anyone. Ibrahim Shabat personifies the problem of the more than 250,000 Israeli Arabs. Shabat was an angry, embittered young man of twenty when the Palestine War broke out. He was born in Tiberias on the Sea of Galilee, an area allotted to the Jewish State under the provisions of the 1947 UN resolution. Tiberias lay close to the Syrian frontier and after the war the district was declared a closed area by the Israeli Government. By then some 80 percent of Israel's Arab citizens were living under a military administration. In a case like that of Ibrahim's family, this meant that the military governor of the northern region was able to refuse them permits to return home from Nazareth where they had sought safety during the war. The permits were refused "on grounds of security." The minister of agriculture then decreed that the family's land was "uncultivated." Since he had the right to ensure that the land was cultivated, he could turn it over to any other party for this purpose. Neighboring Jewish colonies took up the "uncultivated" land.

Ibrahim's only consolation for this high-handed treatment on

the part of the government was the fact that 40 percent of the
land owned by Arabs living in Israel was expropriated in similar
fashion. When compensation was paid (it often was not), payment
was made at a time when the Israeli pound was worth a quarter
of its previous value and on the basis of 1950 market prices
which that year were at a record low.

Ibrahim remained a staunch Arab nationalist even after he
became a citizen of Israel. But as the years passed he was ever
more concerned with the fate of the Arab minority under the
military administration. He learned Hebrew which he now
teaches in Arab schools. He joined the Mapam party and became
editor of its Arabic magazine, *al-Mirsad.*

I met him in Nazareth in September 1967. He was tall, with
flecks of gray hair on his temples. He looked older than his
forty years. As we sat one evening at the house of a mutual
friend, Ibrahim told me he had joined Mapam because, apart
from the Communists, it was the one group which showed genuine
concern for the Arab minority and some courage in fighting for
their rights. He said: "I came to believe that the best chance
for improving our condition lay in the political process. I regard
myself a Zionist for there is nothing incompatible with being an
Arab and holding Zionist ideals. But the Zionism practiced by
the present regime controlled by the Mapai party is tantamount
to racial discrimination and, in fact, the relations between Arab
and Jew have not improved because of it. We are considered
strangers in our own land."

He reserved his bitterest sentiments for Ben Gurion who, he
felt, had singlehandedly done more to destroy the Israeli Arab
faith in Zionist Government. "Once when I met with Ben Gurion
he told me that Israel is the land of the Jewish people and only
of the Jews. 'You Arabs,' he said, 'can enjoy the same minority
rights here as any other minority group in the world, but you have
to face the fact that you live in a Jewish country.' "

Ibrahim Shabat was a broken man who had struggled to
find a measure of dignity for his people in an atmosphere which
accorded them none. He was not alone.

Aida M____ was an attractive young woman, a social worker.
She spoke to me with a simple intensity about her own impressions.
"You must understand that this is not a question of Arab and

Jew. We can and do get along. We have good relations with some
Jewish families in Upper Nazareth; many ordinary citizens we
know are shocked and sympathetic when they discover the
conditions under which we live — with the military government
and all it implies. The greatest barrier is perhaps the Jewish
ignorance of us as a people and a community, and how we live.
Indifference is worse and there is plenty of that too. Worst of
all, however, is the negative attitude, the destructive activities
of some of the rulers of this country, beginning with Ben Gurion.
The military government which he initiated was only abolished
in December 1966, but we know that it can be reimposed. For
eighteen years we have lived in isolation from the mainstream
of Israeli life and consequently Israelis, through no real fault
of their own, forget we exist. Many have fought with us to gain
us more freedom and for this we are grateful. But the ruling
elite set a powerful example for the majority of its citizens, and
for many Arabs it is difficult to distinguish between the actions
of the government and the attitudes of the Jews. We have proven
our loyalty to the land of our forefathers, but the government
has never earned our faith in it."

The system of laws upon which the military government was
founded was not, in fact, an Israeli invention but rather a device
which the British Mandatory used first against the Arabs during
the Rebellion of 1936, and thereafter against Jewish terrorists in
1945. There was, however, a certain irony in the way in which it
came to be used against the Arab minority in Israel. At a Jewish
lawyers' conference held in Tel Aviv in February 1946, many men
who were later to rise to prominent positions in the Israeli
Government denounced the Mandate Defense Laws in the
strongest possible terms. The conference passed a resolution
which noted that the laws "undermine law and justice and
constitute a grave danger to the life and liberty of the individual
and establish a rule of violence without any judicial control."[10]
Jacob Shapiro, who later became Israeli attorney general and then
minister of justice, declared that even Nazi Germany had not
witnessed a comparable system of laws. Yet it was this same
system, together with its military courts, which the Israeli Government adopted for its Arab citizens.

The organizational structure of the military government is

quite simple. Under Israeli Defense Laws (1949) pertaining to
security areas, the minister of defense appointed military
governors for three principal areas: Galilee, the Triangle bordering
on Jordan and the Negev, known respectively as the Military
Governments North, Central and South. The military governor
has extensive powers over the lives of the Arabs who live
under his jurisdiction ranging from detention for up to one year
without trial or charge, to permanent banishment, confiscation
or destruction of property, billeting soldiers and police at the
inhabitants' expense and the imposition of curfews. Under Article
125 of the laws large portions of the military government covering
most of the northern, all the central and one district of the
southern region were declared "closed" areas. This is one of the
most oppressive articles in the laws, for the entry into and exit
from the closed areas are controlled by means of permits. Freedom
of movement can be severely restricted. An Arab who wants
to travel outside his village or town must apply for a military
permit before he can leave. The permits designate the purpose
of the trip and the route to be traveled. No stopovers are
allowed. Jewish colonies en route are off limits and the bearer
is allowed outside his own area only between the hours of 6 a.m.
and 3 p.m. Permits could be refused without reason.[111]

A military court was the only competent body to try offenders
of the regulations. The court's verdict could not be questioned for,
until 1963, there was no appeal to any civil authority. After that
date, appeals could be made to the supreme court but the court,
as a general rule, would not interfere with the actions of the
military government. The military courts were not obliged to
divulge the nature of a security offense, for this itself would be
a breach of security.

The Israeli military establishment consistently defended the
system on security grounds. In the early days of the State there
was unquestionably a need for the apparatus of the military
government to watch closely those citizens whose loyalty was open
to question. It soon became apparent to the Arabs, and some
sections of the Israeli public, however, that the military government was serving interests other than those strictly connected
with the security of the State. Like power groups anywhere, the
military government had a vested interest in the status quo. The

extent of its activities and influence was immense as the state controller noted in his report on the Ministry of Defense in 1959: "The military government interferes in the life of the Arab citizen from the day of his birth to the day of his death. It has the final say in all matters concerning workers, peasants, professional men, merchants, educated men, education and social services. The military government interferes in the registration of births, deaths, and even marriages of the population, in land affairs, and the appointment and dismissal of teachers and civil servants. Often too, it arbitrarily interferes in the affairs of the political parties, political and social activities and the affairs of local and municipal councils."[112] The military governor was, in George Orwell's phrase, Big Brother to the Arab; he could be benevolent or tyrannical, but in either case the Arab was at the mercy of his personal judgment.

The military went unchallenged for nearly a decade, until voices of protest began to be heard among opposition political parties and the intelligentsia. By 1962 a vote in the Knesset to retain the military government passed by only three votes; the next year the majority was cut to one vote. The main charge against the system was that there no longer existed any connection between the effective control of the frontiers and the functions of the military government.

Another charge, which the majority of Arabs believed was true, was that the military government had become the private institution of the ruling Mapai party of Ben Gurion. Sabri Jiryis gives his eyewitness account of a visit to an Arab village in Galilee by a representative of the military governor three days before the elections to the Fifth Knesset (1961). The representative told a general meeting of the village that the government wanted the village to vote for one of the Arab lists affiliated with the Mapai. The election was supervised in such a way as to ensure the "loyalty" of the inhabitants. In another incident, which reached the supreme court, it was established that the military had interfered in the elections of a local council by issuing expulsion orders for two elected members deemed "undesirable" to the military.[113]

The Arab view is colored by an intense suspicion of the Mapai party in particular and of Zionism in general, largely because it is seen to affect them directly. For example, whenever an area has been declared "closed" this has, in many cases, been a prelude to land expropriation and Jewish settlement. In 1962, Shimon Peres, then deputy minister of defense, observed that "it is by making use of Article 125, on which the military government is to a great extent based, that we can directly continue to struggle for Jewish settlement and Jewish immigration... If we are agreed that settlement has a far-reaching political import, we must prevent the creation of a fait accompli (i.e. further Arab settlement) incompatible both with the Zionist concept of the State of Israel and with the law."[141] To the Arab there seemed no end to the process of erosion.

Over the years the military government succeeded only in strengthening the very disaffection it was designed to counteract. It placed a physical barrier between Arab and Jew. Also, it symbolized a far more traumatic reality, namely, the sudden and violent transformation of the Arab community into a defenseless minority. And more, it symbolized the Palestinian's loss of his struggle for national liberation to the alien forces which now firmly ruled the country. He could not identify with the European in control, and the image of the free man across the frontier filled his mind. As an Arab he identified with his brethren in surrounding countries. Emotionally he could remain with the Arab majority of the Middle East, but in day-to-day reality he was fenced into his minority lot. Intense psychological alienation went with his physical isolation, without any compensating factors permitting the development of a national pride, be it Arab or Israeli. Television and radio brought his fellow Arab into his Israeli home from Lebanon, Syria, Jordan and Egypt, but he could not communicate back.

All these factors added to the centrifugal forces tugging him toward the outer perimeter of Israeli life, while the military government seemed designed to keep him there. Israel was the promise of democracy and equality for all which, in time, might have drawn the Arab toward the center. Israel, however, fulfilled the promise with the military government and land expropriation. Hence, democracy became a lie. To the Arab, failure to find a job in the urban Jewish labor market was discrimination; failure to find a place in the Hebrew University of Jerusalem was discrimination; the lack of educational facilities was discrimination. And so it went in all phases of life. Even when there was goodwill on the Jewish side, the Arab was quick to take offense. Sincerity to him was hypocrisy, understanding was paternalism or condescension, indifference was just indifference and hostility was mutual.

By the same token the existence of the military government reinforced the already strong insular attitudes of the Jewish community which were carried over from the mandate period. The Jewish National Home had not been intended for the benefit of the Arab and so the Jewish State was not meant specifically to cater to his particular needs. As for the military government, it was not there to punish crimes the Arabs *had* committed, but for the offenses which they *might* commit if they were not kept in their place. The argument would run: well, as long as the military government is maintained there must be good reason for it. Simplistic reasoning is comforting and relieves the need for deeper and more sympathetic reflection. The stereotype of the Arab remains intact; he is "one of them" and, as such, potentially dangerous. The abolition of the military system was greeted as the triumph of liberalism. It was also the victory for the cooler counsels of expediency. Either way the basic challenge of a non-Jewish minority was left unresolved. For could the Zionists force the pace of Arab assimilation when, in principle, they had consistently opposed Jewish assimilation in the Diaspora?

Nevertheless, within the general democratic framework of Israeli society there were channels through which protest against the injustices of the military government could be made. In Israel's early years, Arab political opposition was neither highly organized, nor articulate, despite the unusually high percentage of Arabs voting in Knesset elections, indicating a keen interest in political issues. In the first place there were no Arab political parties which could galvanize political opinion. After the Palestine War no effective Arab leadership was left in the country. It was several years before the community emerged from the state of shock suffered as a result of the defeat, and adapted itself to the radical new circumstances under which it now lived. In addition, all existing parties in the new state represented various shades of the Zionist ideology and it was unlikely that Arabs could identify with the political views in this spectrum. Moreover none of the major Jewish parties encouraged or even desired Arab membership in their factions.

The sole exception was the Communist party, Maqi, which shortly after the war combined both the Arab and Jewish factions which had operated openly during the Mandate. Maqi has been the only non-Zionist party in Israel to struggle consistently for Arab minority rights. It fought vigorously against discriminatory provisions of the Nationality Law which was complementary to the Law of Return. Under the provisions of the latter law, the right of immigration and citizenship by "return" was conferred on Jews all over the world. Arab residents of Israel, on the other hand, had to prove that they had been citizens of Palestine, which in practice was not easy owing to the very small number of Palestinians who possessed passports or identity cards. Communists also took up the cry against arbitrary arrests, expulsions and destruction of Arab villages, expropriation and the like. Fulminations were directed at the government for their handling of the Kafr Qassim incident, a tragedy which left a deep imprint on the minds of Palestinians in Israel and elsewhere.

On the eve of the Israeli invasion of Egypt on October 29, 1956, a curfew was imposed on several villages in the Little Triangle near the Jordanian border.[151] The Triangle had been under permanent night-time curfew since 1948, but on this occasion it was to be strictly enforced from 5 p.m. to 6 a.m. The village authorities only heard of the curfew a half hour before it was to begin and protests were made to the unit commander that the workers in the fields and nearby villages or more distant spots would have no way of knowing of the curfew. The Mukhtar was assured that all the workers would be allowed safe conduct to their homes. However, in the first hour of the curfew, as the sun was gently setting behind the hills, the men of the Israeli Frontier Force shot forty-nine men, women and children of Kafr Qassim as they returned to their homes. Some weeks passed before the Israeli public became aware of the details. The prime minister ordered an inquiry. Eleven members of the border police were finally brought to trial when the full course of the tragic events came to light.

The recorded testimony of the district court tells, among other events, of the arrival of a lorry at the edge of the village at about half past five. It carried four men and fourteen women aged from twelve to sixty-six years. The dead bodies of nearly two dozen villagers were already scattered by the roadside. Soldiers ordered the driver to pull up and get out. The women had seen the bodies of their fellow villagers and they implored the soldier in command to allow them to stay in the lorry. The soldier ignored their entreaties and their identity cards, and told them to get down. As the men and women lined up beside the lorry the soldier, who had been joined by others, opened fire and continued to shoot until all eighteen persons were dead, or appeared to be dead. A girl of fourteen, Hannah Amer, who had been hit in the head and leg, was the sole survivor.

Almost two years to the day after this incident, the court handed down its judgment. The two chief accused, a major and a lieutenant, were given seventeen and fifteen years respectively. Other sentences ranged from fifteen to seven years, and three men were acquitted. The Kafr Qassim incident shocked the whole nation, although some of the Israeli press, including the right-wing nationalist papers *Herut* and *Lamerhav,* attacked the court for the harshness of the sentences. For the Arabs, the most numbing shock of the affair was the gradual reduction of the terms of imprisonment of the convicted men until the last of them was released just three and a half years after the affair itself. The brigadier who had given the original orders for the curfew and the methods to be used in implementing it was tried by another court and found guilty of a "technical error." He was fined one piastre.

The Kafr Qassim affair impressed upon the Arab minority the extreme precariousness of their position both in terms of security and justice. A young Arab medical student from Haifa explained to me what he believed to be the real significance of Kafr Qassim: "The effect was greatest on the younger generation, people like myself. Our parents could forgive, although they could not forget. We can do neither. We Arabs who were born in Israel, or who can remember nothing else, know no other country but this one. Our defeat in the Palestine War was because of mismanagement by our leaders.

Kafr Qassim happened because there was, at a certain moment, a set of circumstances, an atmosphere which permitted that atrocity to take place. That atmosphere was created by men like one of the defendants at the trial who declared with all frankness that he had always considered us as an enemy within the State. The atmosphere was also created by our own community, because we chose to demonstrate our loyalty to this country through subservience to the masters. As long as we are subservient we will have no real freedom."

He was reflecting on the main characteristic of Arab political life since 1948, which was a kind of paternalistic relationship between Ben Gurion's Mapai party and the Arab community. Mapai did not admit Arabs into its membership, but at election time attempted to reach the Arab electorate indirectly through affiliated Arab lists. The lists were carefully prepared to include rich notables in the large towns, men who had a vested interest in the status quo, who had retained their traditional authority in the local communities and who could dispense patronage through their connections with the government. The strategy was successful and the Arab lists brought considerable support to Mapai in the Knesset. This did not necessarily reflect the real attitudes of Arab voters toward the government, for their support of the Mapai party (traditionally the strongest) was not out of conviction that this would bring changes in the regime, but out of fear that through pressure from the military government the ruling party could make known its favor or displeasure. The Arab Members of the Knesset (MK) affiliated to Mapai were regarded as rubber stamps for the government's policy. The view was justified, if only for the reason that these MKs voted in parliament in 1962 and 1963 for the continuation of the military government.

Mapam is a left of center Zionist party which admitted Arabs to the party after 1954. Mapam tried to foster its image among the Arabs as their friend and champion, although it had shown ambivalent tendencies toward the Arab minority resulting from its Zionist orientation. However, Mapam had contributed a good deal to the material welfare of the Arab community through party-run kibbutzim and other organizations. It had also provided the Arabs with a platform of protest in its magazine *al-Mirsad* which, unlike the Histadrut backed *al-Yaum* (Today), does not attempt to window-dress government policy. Mapam never had the appeal of the Communist Maqi party, however, owing to the greater ideological independence of the latter and the fact that Mapam compromised its image by joining coalitions with Mapai. Maqi's proportion of the popular Arab vote has been second only to Mapai-supported lists, and has been much stronger than Mapam, especially in the towns and villages.

A significant development occurred before the elections to the Sixth Knesset in 1965. Maqi split into two groups, the offshoot Raqah party forming an Arab Communist group, although about 30 percent of its membership was Jewish. The split had been smoldering for several years and was based in part on ideological grounds. Maqi has always held that the Arabs should enjoy absolutely equal rights with the Jews as a national minority within Israel. Raqah, on the other hand, considers the Arabs of Israel to be part of the Palestinian Arab nation and the vanguard in the struggle to win and maintain their rights. Through its party organ, *Unity*, a bi-weekly paper and the best edited Arabic newspaper in Israel, Raqah made its appeal to Arab voters as a non-Zionist Arab party. The party's results were impressive as it outscored Mapai in the towns and virtually wiped Maqi off the map as a political force among the Arabs. Raqah also gained two seats in the Knesset.

An earlier rift within Maqi dating back to 1958, produced in 1960 an all-Arab nationalist group known as al-Ard (The Earth). After long and bitter litigation with Israeli authorities, the movement was outlawed as subversive.

Hence the importance of Raqah becomes even greater, because as Sabri Jiryis, one of the founders of al-Ard concludes pessimistically: "it can be assumed that the official Israeli policy of suppressing any manifestation of the nationalist movement among the Arabs resident in Israel, and of combatting any organization that claims to defend their rights, will continue unchallenged."[116] There is justification for this apprehension. The chief of Mapai's Department of Arab Affairs declared in 1966 that the existence of an Arab party which was not allied to a Jewish party was a threat to the State. His reasoning was that Arab nationalist parties eventually throw up extremist elements and it would be a disaster for Israel and her Arab citizens to allow a party to exist which did not identify with the State.

From the Israeli viewpoint, the conflict between Zionist ideology and any modern Arab movement of liberation must be irrevocable.

PART THREE

11

Aftermath of the Six Day War

Early on the morning of June 5, 1967, Israeli Mirage jets, flying in groups of four, skimmed across the silent waters of the Mediterranean and slipped under the protective beams of Egyptian radar. Within hours every Egyptian airfield looked as if it had been struck by the plague. Runways were pockmarked with bomb craters and scarred by grotesque heaps of metal which, the night before, had been MiG fighter planes. The Six Day War ended then and there.

Sighs of relief went up around the world. Embattled Zion was safe. The weeks of tension prior to the war had been climaxed by President Nasser's request for the removal of United Nations troops from northern Sinai and from Sharm al-Shaykh on the Straits of Tiran. In their stead he moved up units of the Egyptian Army, perhaps genuinely fearful at the time of an imminent Israeli attack against Syria although evidence for this has subsequently been found wanting.

In Israel the fear was no less real that Nasser's moves were but a prelude to invasion. In a preemptive strike, Israel was now triumphant, her enemies' armies strewn across the steaming deserts in tattered shreds. So decisive was the Israeli victory, so crushing the Arab defeat that the hope was confidently expressed: "Surely now, peace is possible." Israel's one-eyed general, Moshe Dayan smilingly told reporters: "I'm just waiting for the telephone to ring from Amman and Cairo." King Hussein had lost half his kingdom and it was thought he could quickly be brought to terms. The late President Nasser had lost half his army and would naturally want a speedy settlement. "Try us," said Israel to her Arab neighbors, "try us, and you will see how generous we can be."

Almost as soon as the guns fell silent along the cease-fire lines and the dust settled on the battlefield, the moment of optimism passed. The hot war gave way to weeks of incessant, badgering debate in the United Nations Security Council which attempted to hammer out a political solution. Five weary months after hostilities ended a compromise of sorts was reached by the Security Council in its resolution of November 22, 1967. The bitterly partisan debate left the Council's image much tarnished, as the U.S.S.R. vigorously supported the Arab position and the U.S.A. defended the Israeli side. Cynics again wondered about the effective purpose of this international forum and practically no one was prepared to claim that politics was still the art of the possible. The reaction of the Arab governments and of Israel to the Council's resolution confirmed the suspicion that it was, after all, an exercise in futility.

The resolution rests upon two, necessarily related, principles. The second paragraph of the introduction stresses (1) "the inadmissibility of the acquisition of territory by war," and (2) "the need to work for a just and lasting peace in which every state in the area can live in security."

In accepting the resolution, the Arab governments emphasize the first part of the statement and consequently demand the complete withdrawal of Israeli troops from *all* occupied territory. As she has in the past, Israel stresses her demand for security implying the need for *more* territory. The two sides are therefore deadlocked on matters of principle from which no bargaining positions have either been adopted or even seem possible. I.F. Stone gave the best description of the impasse in these words: "If God is dead, he surely died trying to solve the Arab-Israeli conflict."

The traumatic effects of the war on both sides, for the Israelis the anguish of their peril and for the Arabs the humiliation of their defeat, form an intangible barrier to peace in the short run. Present fears and suspicions are fed by vivid memories of past conflicts none of which can be simply banished by official statements of future peaceful intent.

To date, however, the fatal flaw in any proposed political settlement, from whatever quarter, has been the failure to come to grips with circumstances which have been radically altered by the war with the emergence of new and vitally important political forces in the area. The Six Day War acted as a catalyst for a movement among the Palestinian people which has sent down young but hardy roots into a soil rich and fertile for revolution. Palestinian commando forces, which have burgeoned into a full-scale national liberation movement, would appear to make nonsense of proposals to solve the Palestine "refugee problem." As never before, the heart of the conflict in the Middle East is clearly shown to be the Palestinians' continuing struggle against the encroachment of Zionism. To the Palestinians, therefore, the Security Council resolution is not a compromise, but a sellout. In the future, Palestinian revolutionaries are likely to make life as uncomfortable for the Arab governments as for the Israelis.

Shortly after the end of the war, the late President Nasser announced the conditions for peace which he felt both his own people and the Israelis might accept. "I want a settlement with Israel," he said, "but not unconditional surrender. So far, Israel has only offered us terms of surrender." As quid pro quo for an Israeli withdrawal from occupied territories, Nasser was prepared to offer:

1. A declaration of non-belligerence;
2. The recognition of the right of each country to live in peace;
3. The recognition of the territorial integrity of all countries, including Israel;
4. Secure boundaries;
5. Freedom of navigation on international waterways;
6. A just solution to the Palestine refugee problem.

Nasser was anxious for a settlement out of fear that time would sanctify the Israeli occupation. In February 1970, he reiterated his position on a peace settlement. On the question of the Palestinians, he said that the refugees themselves should be given the choice of either repatriation to Israel or compensation for lost property. A referendum held under United Nations auspices could determine the will of the people. The president admitted, however, that as long as peace appeared beyond immediate reach, it would soon be impossible to convince the Palestinian organizations of the prudence of this course. "What choice would I then have," he said, "but to support these courageous people in their resistance?"

Nasser also had his own security problem to worry about. The Six Day War left Israel in full command of the skies, and gave her the capability to strike at any point inside Egypt with impunity. The Bar Lev Line, named after the Israeli chief of staff, marks the forward defense position along the west bank of the Suez Canal. Almost daily air raids were successful in knocking out Egyptian surface-to-air missile sites. This development, in turn, obliged the Russians to introduce the more sophisticated SAM III missiles which are designed to bring down warplanes flying below 2,500 feet.

As with American air strikes over North Vietnam, Israeli warplanes have taken their toll of civilian lives. On February 12, 1970, a scrap-metal factory at Abu Zabal near Cairo was hit, killing over seventy persons and wounding another hundred. The Israeli Defense Ministry called the strike an "accident" leaving many Israelis incredulous. "We don't make mistakes like that," one young woman told a reporter, "there was probably a good military reason for hitting that factory." Israelis too, it would seem, have become victims of their own image of invincibility.

Nasser, therefore, remained adamant on Israeli withdrawal from Sinai. "I always talk of a political solution," he said, "but as long as Israel continues its three-year occupation, I believe it is our duty to liberate the occupied territories." Negotiations could be carried on through the United Nations, not face to face as Israel insists, for this would be tantamount to unconditional surrender.

At a conference on international affairs in the Hague early in 1970, Foreign Minister Abba Eban met the late President Nasser's argument head on, denouncing him for his total lack of sincerity. He repeated his government's demand for direct negotiations leading to formal peace treaties with each Arab neighbor. Except to say that Israel must enjoy secure and recognized frontiers, Eban refused to speculate on what they might or should be. Palestinians could not be a party to any negotiations as they had not been involved in the war. And more recently in the Israeli Parliament he observed that the concept of a Palestinian entity was both "sterile and ambiguous."

The best approach to the refugee problem, in Eban's mind, would be to call an international conference to draft a plan for the resettlement of Palestinians in Arab lands with international aid. "No refugee will be permitted to return to Israel," he added.

Each side proclaimed the possibility of peace while at the same time advancing conditions for peace which were mutually exclusive. Nasser's formula had the virtue of substance although he might have pondered more carefully beforehand the consequences of a war for which he was ill-equipped and unprepared. It is impertinent for the vanquished to ask the victor to relinquish the spoils of war! The beleaguered president may, however, have taken solace in the frustration of Israeli soldiers who manned the Bar Lev Line. Said one soldier returning from the Suez front: "The dirtiest trick Nasser played on us was allowing Sinai to be captured. The heat and desolation there will get us before he does."

Israeli policy makers have often demonstrated a strong penchant for avoiding the heart of the chronic Middle East crisis, preferring instead to deal with the fringes. Accordingly, Israelis have regarded Cairo (and through it, Moscow) as the key to peace. The Palestinians, as mere refugees, constitute a humanitarian, not a political problem. The commandos are a tool of Egypt's war of attrition against Israel and therefore Cairo, and the other Arab governments must bear the responsibility for their activities. Israelis then argue, mistakenly, that the commandos have no autonomous will and that the resistance will wither away once Egypt is forced to submit. The Israeli attitude is inherited from deeply ingrained Zionist patterns of thought and action concerning the Palestinians. During the years of the British Mandate Zionists firmly believed that, if London and Washington backed their program, Palestinians need never be consulted and would eventually come around to accepting their fate. The reason for the persistence of such attitudes, so simple that it bears repetition, is that Jewish statehood and Palestinian self-determination are but two sides of the same coin. However, one side of a coin cannot be erased simply by turning it face down. For Israel to squarely come to grips with the Palestinians, it would mean confronting and destroying myths about them which Israel has helped create and perpetuate. This in turn would create an intolerable strain upon the Zionist psyche and an unbearable sense of guilt. And guilt is something which Zionists demand of others, not of themselves.

Hence, despite Israel's insistence that "everything is negotiable" in eventual peace talks, her actions since the Six Day War are out of line with that declared policy and seem perversely calculated to ensure the continuation of the conflict for decades to come.

The status of Jerusalem, the Israelis say, is not negotiable. The Jordanian sector, or East Jerusalem, has been "liberated" and the Holy City reunited to become the eternal capital of Israel. Steps were quickly taken after the war to integrate the two Jerusalems. The barbed wire and concrete barriers were dismantled. Signs in Hebrew appeared all over the Arab sector and the Arab municipal administration was combined with the Jewish — minus the Arab mayor, however, who was banished from his city and his country for publicly opposing the Israeli annexation. The Arabs of Jerusalem were bitter over this move. "We're so integrated," one of them told me, "that we now have prostitutes in our city for the first time."

No doubt the Israelis are determined to stay. One of the government's first acts was to raze to the ground the homes of some 200 families who lived beside the Wailing Wall in order to create a plaza for more visitors and worshipers. It was here, next to the site of the ancient Temple, that the Israeli Army held a vast victory celebration. The Arab inhabitants of the quarter were given a few hours to evacuate before the bulldozers moved in. No compensation was offered for their loss of property. The Israeli Government was also willing to risk worldwide censure for its decision to annex Jerusalem. This has apparently paid off, for the time being at least. As Chief Rabbi Unterman put it: "We cannot believe in international guarantees, only in our possession."

Israel's gain was Jordan's loss measured in terms of the revenue from tourists attracted to the Holy Places. Annexation of the Holy City, however, has not meant that the Arabs of East Jerusalem continue to profit from foreign tourists. Arab hotels have practically no business. Under Israeli law, Arab tourist agencies, bus and taxi companies operate at a disadvantage against their Jewish counterparts.

While in Jerusalem shortly after the June war, I stayed at the new and very beautiful YMCA in the Arab sector. Upper parts of the building had been damaged during the fighting, but repairs had been immediately begun. The only guest in the place, apart from myself and a young couple from Cyprus, was General Odd Bull, the Swedish head of the United Nations Truce Supervision Team.

A few minutes walk from the hotel was the home of Dr. Antoun Atallah, a former Jordanian foreign minister. I went to see him on my first evening in Jerusalem. He was a soft-spoken, elegant gentleman with an intense love for his city, *his* Jerusalem. To my surprise, he said he doubted whether religious or historical sentiment were the main motives for the Israeli conquest (he was quite emphatic about that) of the Old City. He pointed out that Jerusalem was the commercial center of the West Bank. Businessmen, merchants, tradesmen and farmers from all the towns of the West Bank had dealings in Jerusalem. To control it was like having an economic stranglehold on the whole of the West Bank.

The Israeli Government has requisitioned hundreds of acres of private land around East Jerusalem for residential development. The new Jewish quarter of Ramat Eshkol has already been created and some 7,000 housing units will be built over the next three years. Amid this flurry of activity and planning, the economic plight of the Arabs in Jerusalem continues. Immediately after the war, in response to the need, a Beirut-based organization, *The Friends of Jerusalem,* began to raise money in Arab countries and Europe to help finance needy Arab families thus allowing them to remain in Jerusalem. As Dr. Atallah said, it is important to the Arabs that they remain in Jerusalem itself for the duration of the occupation.

The attitude of Jerusalem's Arabs to the municipal elections of October 1969 is an indication of their feeling toward the Israeli Government. Although Israeli spokesmen hailed the Arab turnout as a witness to their benevolent policies, in fact only about 14 percent of the 35,000 eligible voters went to the polling booths. Nor has a single Arab applied for Israeli citizenship.

Early in 1969 the Church of the Holy Sepulchre suddenly became a rallying point for Palestinian discontent. On January 26, twenty-five Palestinian women, Christian as well as Muslim, began a hunger strike in protest against the Israeli occupation. At the entrance to the church, a mother and her daughter handed out leaflets to visitors and passers-by explaining the reasons for the strike. The two were arrested, which only reinforced the strike when a number of other women, some of them quite elderly, joined those already inside. The strike embarrassed Israeli authorities who had tried to make out that the Arab population was content with the annexation of the Holy City. An Orthodox priest finally intervened and arranged for the strike to be called off on condition that the arrested women were released.

In other occupied areas, in Gaza, the Golan Heights and the West Bank, the Israeli Government is consciously creating new realities, or "new facts." They put a question mark on Abba Eban's grand phrase that "everything is negotiable." The average Israeli, open and frank in the best spirit of a pioneer society, is amused. The current joke appreciated by Israelis runs like this: "Certainly Israel wants peace; a piece of Syria, a piece of Jordan, a piece of Egypt..." Confronting the opponent with a fait accompli was a familiar pattern of Zionist strategy during the Mandate years. Given the nature of the Zionist program as an "all-or-nothing" venture, the strategy was perfectly understandable. Today, part of Israel's tragedy is that she is unable to look beyond the establishment of a military victory, for the policy of the continuing fait accompli demands the complete capitulation of an enemy which refuses to submit, or the disappearance of a people who stubbornly assert their will to exist as a community.

The "new facts" are visible in the Golan Heights of Syria. Before the June war there were about 123,000 Syrians living in this area. Now there are about 5,000 persons, mainly of the Druze sect who stayed in the area around Majd al-Shams. The city of Qunaytra had only fourteen inhabitants after the war and some eighty villages to the south are practically empty. To date the International Red Cross has received more than 739 applications from Syrians wishing to go back on urgent compassionate grounds to rejoin a wife, a husband or an aged relative. Israel has allowed only eighty-three persons to return. Meanwhile, 15,000 Jewish settlers are slowly establishing military kibbutzim on the frontier. On March 21, 1969, the deputy director of the Jewish Agency's Settlement Department, Avraham Rosenmann, announced a proposal for forty new settlements in the Heights. Twenty-two were already built and plans were in the works for a city of 50,000 inhabitants. The foundation stone of one town, Ramat Shalom, was laid on April 23 of that year.

As in all the occupied territories, Israelis have "persuaded" Arabs to leave by various methods of intimidation and collective punishment against villagers. The Gaza Strip is no exception and it is unlikely that it will be given up in any future peace settlement. The Strip contains eleven refugee camps and over 250,000 refugees who greatly outnumber the indigenous inhabitants. For twenty years before the June war, these Palestinians lived at just above subsistence level from international charity doled out through the United Nations. A day-by-day existence corroded their hope, but intensified their longing to return to their homeland and turned them into bitter Palestinian nationalists.

During the Six Day War the Israeli Army encountered stiff resistance from untrained, ill-equipped but desperate Palestinians in the Strip. The occupation troops quickly sensed the depth of bitterness among these Arabs but the Israelis' outspoken contempt for them scarcely made them capable of comprehending such emotion. The contempt was returned by bitter hatred until the tension broke all bonds of restraint and the military government freely wielded the iron fist of repression. To control the hostile population, the military authorities adopted arbitrary curfews and arrests as well as indiscriminate demolition of civilian houses.

A minor incident in January 1968, brought matters to a head. One day a small homemade bomb went off in the Gaza fish market. No one was hurt. The culprit was said to have made his escape along the beach in the direction of a refugee camp. There his fellow Arabs closed about him like a silent anonymous sea. In reprisal, the Israelis blew up several fishermen's storehouses and destroyed some fishing boats. As additional retaliation total curfew was imposed on the camp for five days and nights.

For twenty-eight hours no one was allowed to leave his house on any pretext. This was a particularly trying punishment, for none of the houses contained a latrine. A British observer, Michael Adams, reported that "on the second day the curfew was lifted for an hour at UNRWA's urging to allow refugees to collect water. They were still forbidden to leave camp and no distribution of food was allowed; not many managed to get water. During the break all men between sixteen and sixty were ordered onto the compound on the seashore where they were held for seven hours during one of the winter's severest storms while Israeli guards repeatedly fired small arms over their heads."

In other camps similar punishment was meted out for similar incidents. At the Jabiliyeh camp the male population was gathered and held outdoors for twenty-five hours without food or water. This was in reprisal for the mining of a civilian car causing injury to its three occupants who, it was later revealed, were Israeli smugglers transporting contraband cigarettes and figs. Why Jabiliyeh camp was singled out for punishment remained a mystery.

These measures convinced the Arabs of the Strip that the Israelis were systematically setting out to induce the Palestinians to leave Gaza as a preliminary to its annexation. In 1969 five new military kibbutzim were built at the southern end of the Strip and in northern Sinai, so that the entire Gaza enclave is now surrounded by Jewish settlements. A report carried in the semi-official Cairo daily *al-Ahram* on March 10, 1970, said that the Israeli Government was meeting to discuss a plan to transfer the 300,000 inhabitants of the Strip to the West Bank in order to eliminate guerilla agitation in the area. Two days later, Israel's Minister of Transport Ezer Weizman commented that no decision had been taken on such a plan. In any event, over 30,000 Palestinians had left the Strip in the first weeks after the June war only to add to the swelling numbers of refugees in Jordan.

At its best, Gaza City, hot and squalid, is the kind of festering sore which gives military authorities nightmares. Israel's particular nightmare in Gaza is the militant schoolgirl. A few days after the affair at the Holy Sepulchre in Jerusalem, a crowd of about 3,000 schoolgirls demonstrated for the release of three schoolmates who had been arrested for allegedly harboring a Fateh commando. The demonstration got out of hand when the girls mobbed Israeli armored vehicles and the soldiers turned upon them with their guns and batons. Ninety-three girls were wounded, forty of whom were detained in hospital with broken limbs and other injuries. In an effort to cool the situation the Israelis released the three girls from their confinement. A week later the troops were at it again, this time breaking up a demonstration of stone-throwing schoolboys. In October, a graduation ceremony at the Palestine High School erupted into an anti-Israeli demonstration and several Israeli journalists were caught by flying rocks. The school was immediately commandeered by the army for "military purposes." As a result of almost constant disturbances the military officials have felt obliged to deport nearly sixty teachers from Gaza for alleged incitement to violence. Six other prominent Palestinians were banished to a Bedouin camp in the Sinai for similar offenses.

The West Bank presents only a somewhat less explosive picture. Of the 200,000 refugees who fled the West Bank during the war, only 14,000 of 170,000 who applied have been permitted to return. A Red Cross official in Beirut said, "unofficially," that the Israelis adopted various tactics to ensure that as few refugees as possible would return. For example, after an application was approved by the Israeli side, Red Cross workers often had only a few hours in which to locate the individuals or families concerned who then had to be taken to the crossing point at a specific time. In the chaos of the new refugee camps it was literally impossible to reach applicants soon enough. Some had moved on to Amman and could not be found. Another delay tactic used was to split families by approving the applications of some members while rejecting others, usually those of the teen-aged males. Heads of families would naturally choose to keep their children together and forego the chance for repatriation. Nevertheless, it was an effective, albeit subtle, form of enforced exile.

Other West Bank inhabitants were exiled in more direct fashion. Several villages located along the 1949 armistice lines, such as Zeita, Beit Nuba, Yalu, Amwas, Emmaus and Beit Jala were totally destroyed and the villagers (numbering more than 5,000) dispersed. The Israeli Army took these measures, in each case after the village had surrendered, and, in the case of Zeita at least, *after* the United Nations cease-fire went into effect. At half past six one morning the villagers of Zeita were assembled together and kept all day under the blistering 100-degree June sun while Israeli soldiers demolished sixty-seven homes plus a school and a clinic run by the International Council of Churches. At six that evening the commander appeared with a loudspeaker and told the villagers they could "return to their homes." The fertile land of three villages, Yalu, Beit Nuba and Emmaus (more than 3,000 acres) is now being cultivated and harvested by Israeli farmers.

There is surprisingly little visible evidence that the West Bank is under military occupation. Road signs, of course, appear in Hebrew. This does not worry the Palestinians as much as the fact that biblical names are used rather than current ones: Nablus, for example, becomes the ancient Shechem. Maps which I saw on display in Tel Aviv bookshops do not refer to the West Bank as a part of Jordan, but rather as Judea and Samaria. Palestinians who are well versed in the ideology of political Zionism fear that this portends the expansion of Israeli frontiers to its "historical boundaries."

The lack of a blatant military presence on the West Bank does not mean that "new facts" are not being created there. Immediately after the June war, the then mayor of Nablus, Hamdi Kan'an felt that all the indications suggested some form of permanent relationship with Israel, although this might not mean outright annexation. It would mean, however, that Palestinians would not have complete control over their own affairs. In October of 1969 Israeli Defense Minister Moshe Dayan stated that Israel was in the West Bank "of right and not of sufferance, to visit, to live and to settle. We must be able to maintain military bases there and we must, of course, be able to prevent the entry of any Arab army into the West Bank." Among the "new facts" being established on the West Bank are a dozen military kibbutzim along the Jordan River, an agricultural settlement called Rosh Tzurim near Hebron and a Jewish quarter (initially of about 250 families) in Hebron itself.

While cooperation exists between the various Arab municipalities and the Israeli authorities, the general feeling of the mass of the population is unmistakable. No one wants to live under occupation. The efforts of individual Israeli officials may be appreciated. So too is the agricultural village set up near Janin, north of Nablus, with the help of the Israeli Ministry of Agriculture. Thirteen refugee families benefit from it. But military occupations are inconvenient everywhere. It is all too human for civilians to attribute to the military government the most evil of intentions for its regulations and injunctions. Bureaucratic blunders can appear diabolical when, in fact, they are simply senseless stupidities. A case in point concerned a young Palestinian student who was preparing to leave for university in the United States. I met him in Ramallah where his father, an Anglican priest, told me that before his son could get his papers from the Israeli authorities he had to sign a document declaring that he renounced his rights to return to his homeland. The boy signed rather than pass up the chance to further his education. To me he said: "I'll be back, no matter how long it takes. This is my country." I wondered to myself if he was now a ready-made commando recruit who would come back across the Jordan with a gun in his hand.

The question of school textbooks also caused unnecessary bitterness. The Israeli educational authorities withdrew many texts from the school curriculum on the grounds that they contained anti-Israeli, anti-Zionist or anti-Jewish references. Texts were either rewritten or replaced by books used in Arab schools in Israel. The Israeli censors were possibly overzealous and hypersensitive. I was able to examine one forbidden book called *The Problem of Palestine* which had been used in Jordan's secondary schools. Here, in a book dealing with the very problem with which Palestinians live every day, was perhaps the place to find anti-Israeli sentiment. The book recounts the illegality of the Mandate based upon the Balfour Declaration and the fact that the Mandate was imposed upon an unwilling people. There is no attempt to justify the Zionist position or to describe the movement in anything but political terms. No derogatory references to Jews as people are to be found. The causes of the 1948 defeat are put down to lack of preparation, weakness and division among the Arabs of Palestine. The Arabs' historical, legal and moral rights are emphasized. The text is simply an explanation of the Arab position to its own people.

The mere existence of a military regime is a source of tension and the population under occupation is naturally faced with intolerable options which set in motion an upward spiral of violence. Following a grenade attack in Hebron (November 4, 1969) in which two Arabs were wounded, Israeli troops confiscated twenty-six shops on the town's main street. A military spokesman said that unless the Arabs in the Hebron area co-operated with the occupation forces life would be made unbearable for them. Arabs in the occupied territories, the spokesman said, had three alternatives: fight the terrorists themselves; assist the Israeli Army to do the job for them by supplying information on terrorist activities; or accept neither of these alternatives and take the consequences. Defense Minister Dayan had earlier made a similar threat to Arab leaders in Nablus (April 2, 1969) after the military governor had received complaints about the treatment of detained prisoners and the blowing up of six suspects' houses. In other words, the occupation regime forbids not only passive resistance and non-cooperation, but demands the active assistance of Palestinians in crushing their own people. The result is ultimately counter-productive to the achievement of security since repression is the swiftest means of radicalizing an entire population.

Moreover, when an occupying power exceeds recognized international norms of behavior toward civilians, the finger of censure is bound to be pointed in its direction. Such a norm is the Civilians Convention of 1949 drafted in Geneva after World War II, and to which Israel and the Arab countries are signatories. The Geneva Convention was intended to give "protected persons" (that is, civilians under occupation) certain fundamental rights which occupying powers were bound to observe. Article 53 prohibits the destruction of property; article 33 prohibits collective punishment and the punishment of an individual who has not personally committed a crime; article 49 prohibits, "regardless of motive," the transportation or deportation of protected persons from the occupied territories and also prohibits the occupying power from transferring its own population into the area it occupies; article 27 provides special protection for women. There was, consequently, sufficient prima facie evidence of Israel's contravention of all these articles (and others) for the United Nations Social, Humanitarian and Cultural Committee to condemn such practices. Then in August 1969, a six-man team appointed by the United Nations Human Rights Commission began its investigations into Israeli treatment of Arab civilians. The team comprised one representative each from Senegal, Austria, Jugoslavia, India, Peru and Tanzania. The Israeli Government rejected any cooperation with the commission and blocked its entry into the occupied zones. It is reasonable to assume that if Israel were fulfilling its obligations under the Civilians Convention it would welcome an impartial fact-finding investigation. Possibly General Dayan's frank revelations in the Israeli Parliament in December of 1969 were felt to be sufficient admission. The general said that 516 buildings had been demolished in the occupied territories and seventy-one persons deported from the West Bank since the June war. Informed neutral observers have placed the demolition figure at around 7,000 buildings and deported persons in the hundreds. Satisfied by the evidence it had been able to gather, the Human Rights Commission condemned the Israeli Government for failing to enforce the provisions of the Geneva Convention.

A vigorous debate concerning the future of the occupied territories has been going on in Israeli Government circles for some time. All factions of the National Coalition are agreed on two points: *first*, that peace will not be bought at the price of endangering security which explicitly means territorial aggrandizement, and *second*, that the Jewish character of Israel must be preserved, which raises complicated questions about the future of the Palestinian population in the occupied zones.

The linking of territorial expansion with the problem of security is an equation central to Zionist political ideology. It might be quite untrue to suggest, as some have, that a master plan for the final shape of the Israeli State exists somewhere in Tel Aviv or Jerusalem. Rather, it has been the Zionist practice to deal pragmatically with new situations as they arise. This has often required, for a given moment, a conflict between official statement and design, or as Christopher Sykes has described in his *Cross Roads to Israel,* a "habit to speak not only in two but in several voices, to run several lines of persuasion at the same time, (producing) a not undeserved reputation in the world for chronic mendacity." Since the June war, and with Israel's evident military superiority over the combined forces of her neighbors, a situation has emerged in which Israeli officials feel less need to be evasive or obscure about their territorial requirements. Many voices are, indeed, still heard across the breadth of the Israeli political spectrum, but the differences between them are becoming barely audible.

The Gahal party, led by the former head of the Irgun terrorist group, Menachem Begin, is committed to a map defined by the "historical boundaries" of Eretz Israel. It advocates, in agreement with the non-partisan Greater Israel Movement, the retention of all conquered land. Another member of Gahal is Ezer Weizman, the flamboyant minister of transport in the Meir government. A nephew of Israel's first president, Chaim Weizmann, he has been the chief architect of the Israeli Air Force since his take-over in 1958. Weizman also sits on the Defense Committee with his better known brother-in-law, Moshe Dayan. Both, of course, are likely contenders for Prime Minister Meir's job when the grandmother of Israeli politics retires, or is no more. Weizman shares with Dayan an attitude toward the Arabs which has been typified as the "white settler mentality": "Give the Arabs a bloody nose from time to time," says Weizman, "and it keeps them from getting too cocky."

As a result of the parliamentary elections of October 1969, Gahal strengthened its position in the cabinet increasing its representation from two to six. The general inclination of the Israeli electorate was toward an entrenchment of the status quo and away from any compromise on the territorial question. Since Golda Meir's Labor Alignment party lost seven seats and also its parliamentary majority, Prime Minister Meir was forced to join with Gahal (which won twenty-six seats) in order to create a widely representative ruling coalition. The presence of such disparate groups in the cabinet, from Gahal on the right to Mapam on the left, is bound to create tensions hindering, if not actually preventing, the government from presenting a peace policy *of substance* with a single voice. On the other hand, the distance separating the "maximalists" (Gahal) from the "mini-malists" (Mapam) on the subject of the conquered lands is such that practically no real estate is left with which to bargain for peace with the Arabs. The previously independent Mapam, which has also been absorbed into the Labor Alignment, advocates the retention of Jerusalem, Gaza, the Golan Heights (where the party has established its own kibbutz), and unspecified parts of the West Bank. Despite real and practical differences between the two political poles, considerations stemming from the lowest common denominator of the Zionist ideological spectrum are clearly paramount. As M. Nessyahu, director of the Labor party's ideological center, Beit Berl, has said: "The longer an Arab-Israeli peace takes to materialize, the closer will Israel's permanent borders be to those produced by the Six Day War."

The only labor leader who has outlined a scheme for the future boundaries is Deputy Prime Minister Yigal Allon. His plan inspired the creation of a "security line" of armed Jewish settlements (Nahal kibbutzim) along the west bank of the River Jordan. A small gap in the center, a kind of open corridor, would link the West Bank with the rest of Jordan. According to this so-called Allon Formula, King Hussein's sovereignty over the West Bank would be, at best, tenuous, and for this reason the king denounced the plan. The Allon Formula is widely accepted in government circles as the best basis for ensuring Israel's security and as a starting point in future peace talks. The only party, in fact, which supported the complete withdrawal of Israeli troops and campaigned in the last elections on this platform was the Arab Communist party. The handful of Jewish intellectuals and journalists who lend their voices to the withdrawal argument are politically impotent and isolated.

The government of Prime Minister Golda Meir is perceptibly more hardline than its predecessor under the guidance of the late Levi Eshkol. Mrs. Meir is a consummate politician and a dedicated leader of her people. The ex-Milwaukee schoolteacher, lacking neither in toughness nor independent judgment, has come to trust and rely upon her number one general, Moshe Dayan, for advice in dealing with the occupied territories. Dayan is the man chiefly responsible for security in these areas. He makes frequent trips to West Bank towns and has met most of the Palestinian leaders. The mayor of a small village near Ramallah (who has since been deported) gives this impression of the general: "He's tough, frank and forthright. You know exactly where you stand with him, but you get the feeling that if you don't play the game according to his rules then you just have to expect the consequences — and they can be pretty vicious. That leaves little room for discussion."

General Dayan claims there is no fundamental difference between him and Allon on the territorial question. But Dayan goes further. Addressing a meeting of the pharmacists' union in Tel Aviv in March 1969, he called for faits accomplis in the occupied territories. "The government," he said, "should determine objectives regarding the settlement and economic integration of these areas in order to reduce the dependence of the Arab population on the Arab states." He went on to say that Israel's presence in the occupied areas would give the impression of being temporary if Egyptian law continued to be administered in Gaza and Jordanian law in Judea and Samaria (that is, the West Bank). Dayan has urged a policy of long-term investment in the occupied territories and he naturally asks: "Can Israel, or Israelis, or Jews, invest in the occupied territories without tying their enterprises there with the Israeli economy, with workers from Israel, with Israeli ownership?" Economic and territorial expansion must, therefore, go hand in hand. At the same time Arab labor could be employed to meet the labor shortage in Israel and already a sort of black market of cheap Arab labor has developed frightening many union leaders because of the danger to Israel of "levantinization."

Moshe Dayan also holds to the paradox, which lies deep within the Zionist ideology, that there can be peace although there can never be complete assimilation between the Jewish and Arab communities. Mutual love is not required, only the prevention of mutual hate. How this would lead to harmonious relations between Arab and Jew is left to the imagination.

The Israeli concern over the demographic problem of absorbing the hundreds of thousands of new Arabs under occupation is very real. Some fear that within a generation, given the higher Arab rate of natural increase, the Arab population would out-number the Jewish. It may be recalled that during the British Mandate it was the Palestinians who feared *they* would be submerged if Jewish immigration were not stopped. Other Israelis argue that their predicament may not be so dangerous. An article appearing in the Israeli newspaper *Ma'ariv* suggested, for example, that a Jewish majority and political control of the country could be maintained even in an "enlarged" Israel containing the conquered territories. The real danger of a high Arab birthrate in the short run lies not in the threat to the Jewish majority, but rather in the threat to the "material basis" of Israel. As the Arab population, the article continued, outgrows the limited agricultural land, "the Arab village will be unable to support its inhabitants, while the Jewish town will not happily adopt them." Jews will not willingly bear the financial burden created by rising Arab unemployment as the Arab contributes less to the State's income while enjoying its benefits. The author's solution is that it is "the duty of the Senate to fight the unnaturally high birthrate among the Arabs."

There is nothing immoral about this, the writer goes on, for if the governments of India or Egypt are free to initiate birth-control campaigns among their citizens, then Israel can do what it will with her Arab population by fighting "with all the means of legislation, propaganda and coercion, against the population explosion which endangers the future of both Arabs and Jews." Having thus singled out the Arabs for special treatment, the author looks to the future: "In the longer run we must act, by appealing to the loyalty and economic sense of the Jews of Israel, to convince them that big families are a prerequisite to their existence. At the same time it must be made clear to the Arabs that they cannot be free to maintain the world's highest birthrate in our small and poor country." Such a policy would secure a Jewish majority forever.

12

From War to Revolution

The six explosive days of June 1967, altered more than the
political map of the region. The war unleashed forces which
caught most observers by surprise. Three years later the
conclusion seems inescapable that the key to future peace is
somehow irrevocably bound to the dramatic reappearance of the
Palestinians. However, one must admit at once that the dimensions
of the Palestinian resistance movement have enormously complicated the whole Middle East scene.

For twenty years the international community paid scant
attention to the political aspects of the Palestine Problem. It is
true that the General Assembly of the United Nations dutifully
reiterated each year the principle by which Palestinian refugees
of the 1948 war be allowed to return to their homes, or be
granted compensation for their losses. No one however, except
perhaps the Palestinians themselves, ever believed that it was
possible to enforce this principle. In the perverseness of time even
the justice of the principle was slowly forgotten. The officials and
workers of the UN Relief and Works Agency were the only
people close enough to the refugees to understand their daily
tragedy and to sense the potential explosiveness bred by growing
discontent and despair. Politically, the flow of international
aid to the refugees was just a means of buying time to keep a
lit fuse from burning down to the powder keg.

In the first years after the Palestine War, Palestinians-in-
exile were overcome by the shock which had befallen their community. The Arab Higher Committee under Hajj Amin Husseini
continued to function in Cairo, but it was so discredited that it
soon died a natural death. Other prominent Palestinians either
retired into obscurity or were absorbed into the political life
of the kingdom of Jordan. As everywhere in the Arab world

after World War II, a younger, educated generation of Palestinians was emerging disillusioned by their elders' handling of the crisis. Yet they too clung to the hope that redress of their grievances would be found in the Arab League and the United Nations. Meanwhile, the Palestinian masses drifted from shock into apathy.

The first blow struck for "the cause" was the pathetic gesture of the youth who assassinated King Abdullah, on a Friday noon in June 1951, as the aging monarch was entering the great mosque of Omar in Jerusalem to perform the sabbath prayers. The king had "betrayed Palestine" by undertaking secret negotiations with the Israelis, news of which had leaked out. As the king fell, dying, he cried out to his assailant: "You have killed me. May God kill you." The king's wish was unfulfilled. God was unlikely to take the life of the boy who was called Mustafa which in Arabic means "The Chosen One"!

Individual acts by Palestinians grew more common but were directed, instead, against Israel. Infiltration into Israeli territory (which, to this day, is usually referred to as "Occupied Palestine") commenced almost immediately from Jordan and the Gaza Strip. The temptation was irresistible as the boundaries were often marked by little more than a shallow furrow in the ground or an iron post. Former lands and property were within sight and easy reach. It was simple to venture into a nearby village to see a friend or relative. Others returned to cultivate a piece of land, to steal tools and machinery or rustle livestock to which they felt entitled. Still others were driven by frustration and bitterness to kill Israeli citizens. Blind vengeance brought its own price, and it was usually high.

Israel's policy of retaliation for these raids was directed first against Jordan. The pattern of infiltration and retaliation dated back to the inter-communal clashes of the Mandate days. Only now units of the regular Israeli Army were put into the field. A spiral of violence was again set in motion until the night of October 15, 1953, when Israeli troops attacked and destroyed the village of Qibya in Jordan, killing sixty-six persons, mostly civilians. This was the culmination of a long series of isolated acts by Palestinians and in direct response to the murder of a woman and child only ten miles from Tel Aviv the night before the Qibya attack. Retaliation on this scale appeared to have the merit of reducing the level of infiltration and the numbers of Israeli casualties. Moreover, in the year and a half following the attack, Jordanian authorities cracked down severely on illegal infiltration and more than 1,000 Palestinians were imprisoned for their attempts. The policy of retaliation, while serving immediate security objectives, was based on the rationale that only through demonstration of its military superiority could the Arabs be prodded into a negotiated settlement. Israel still seems convinced that this policy will eventually pay dividends.

The long-range consideration of securing Arab recognition of Israel's existence was more evident in the retaliatory measures adopted against Egypt. A major attack on Gaza on February 28, 1955, resulted in seventy-six casualties. It was this attack which may have forced the late President Nasser to seek massive arms supplies from Eastern bloc countries, eventually leading to the Czech arms deal of September 1955. More important was the fact that the Gaza raid was the immediate cause of the first appearance of Egyptian-trained Palestinian commandos (fidayin), who were selected from among Gaza's refugees for their intimate knowledge of the Israeli countryside. It was but the merest hint of the shape of events to come.

The Suez Crisis erupted in October 1956. The Israeli Army stormed swiftly through Sinai toward the Suez Canal, occupying the Gaza Strip on the way, while Britain and France intervened to "separate" the Egyptian and Israeli combatants. During the Israeli occupation of Gaza, a swarthy young man of about twenty-seven, together with a handful of like-minded Palestinians, decided to launch a clandestine movement led by Palestinians. This was the nucleus of the Fateh organization and the young man who was to remain unnoticed for another decade was Yassir Arafat.

The Suez Crisis brought home to Palestinians like Arafat a simple truth. The Arab world was weak and divided. Egypt's army was defeated. Both the Arabs' political and military strategies regarding Israel were a patent sham. What help could Palestinians expect from the Arab governments save continuing moral support for their cause? That was important, but not enough. The solution was audaciously simple: ultimately, the struggle for the restoration of their rights would have to be assumed by the Palestinians themselves.

The solution appeared to be sheer insanity. Where amid the wreckage of a torn and battered people was the stuff of which liberation movements are made? Those who had never seen the inside of a tent or a baked-brick hovel, who had gained an education and then a profession, would surely never dedicate themselves to the hazards required. A Palestinian doctor or banker in Beirut, an engineer in Kuwait, a professor in an American university and thousands more like them were satisfied with their lot. For others, self-pity was a soothing remedy against the iniquities of fate. "In those days, each of us was a prisoner of his past," explained a Palestinian student. "We dreamed romantically of returning to our homeland, but no one was prepared to take the first step. Servitude is a state of mind; only *we* could break our chains, and set ourselves free to *plan* the future rather than *dream* about it." Palestinians have been called the "new Jews," scattered throughout the world in their Diaspora, driven from their homeland and determined to return. The chances of fulfillment must seem about as farfetched today (if not more so) as the idea of a Jewish national home did in 1897.

Fateh began its campaign of sabotage in January 1965. Yassir Arafat was now in his late thirties and it had taken nearly a decade to bring the movement this far. Arafat himself was no stranger to guerilla fighting. Born in Jerusalem in 1929, the year of the first major outbreak of violence in Palestine, Arafat, with his father and brothers, had joined an underground organization to defend Arab villages against Haganah assaults in 1947-48. After the Palestine War, he began studies at the University of Cairo where he was active in the political affairs of Palestinian students. His extracurricular activities in the early nineteen-fifties included training Egyptian and Palestinian student commandos in harassing tactics to be used against British bases in the Suez Canal Zone. Then in 1957, Arafat went to Kuwait where he and his fellow émigrés began building their secret organization. Political work was carried out mainly among Palestinian students in the Arab world, although Fateh cells were set up as far afield as Stuttgart University in Germany.

By 1965 Fateh had to compete with Ahmad Shukayri's Palestine Liberation Organization, founded the previous year at the Arab League Summit Conference in Cairo. The P.L.O. was suspect among Fateh members since real control of it was vested in the Egyptian Government. Operationally, Fateh made a very modest, an even inauspicious beginning. In the thirty months prior to the June war, Israeli sources reported only 122 sabotage operations. Israeli casualties were low, those of Fateh high. Considering the almost unique situation they faced — difficult and barren terrain unlike the jungles of Vietnam and lack of bases within the territory for which they struggled, as against the Algerian example — a long period of incubation was to be expected. Nevertheless, Fateh was laying the basis for what it now refers to as the Palestine Revolution. It is impossible to say how far, or how rapidly, the revolution would have proceeded without the radical change in circumstances brought about by the June war. There can be no doubt that Israel's occupation of the rest of Palestine, including Old Jerusalem, galvanized Palestinians everywhere to an unprecedented degree of commitment to the reconstruction of their future. Palestine today is in a new state of mind.

In the first weeks after the cease-fire there was little talk of resistance to the occupation among Palestinians on the West Bank. Some people contemplated activism, but did not know how or where to begin. Others naïvely believed that the United Nations would order Israel to withdraw its troops. All were agreed that occupation was intolerable.

A personal encounter will illustrate the suffocating atmosphere of that time. I arrived in Tulkarm on the occupied West Bank in the first week of September 1967, anxious to discover what had become of friends who had been my hosts on a previous journey through that part of Jordan. I was a stranger in town and looked the part. Two little boys approached and greeted me in Hebrew: *"Shalom, Shalom."* They naturally took me for one of the thousands of Israeli tourists who flooded the West Bank after the war. I returned the salutation, and then in Arabic asked them to take me to the house of my friend. Khalid was not at home. During the war he had left for Amman with his wife and three younger children, leaving behind his eldest daughter, her grandmother and an aunt in charge of the house. The banks were closed down after the cease-fire and bank accounts blocked; Khalid hoped to borrow cash from relatives in Amman and return. When he applied through the Red Cross for permission to return, the Israelis approved for his family with the exception of his twelve-year-old son. Khalid is still in Amman teaching at a government high school and, when he is able, he smuggles money to the rest of his family in Tulkarm.

His eldest daughter, Ghida, made me welcome. She was a pretty, plump girl of sixteen with a solemn, gentle disposition. Over coffee she told me the story of her family's experiences during the preceding weeks. "Father took us to Nablus when the war began. It is further back from the border than Tulkarm, and he thought we would be safer there. On June 11, a friend brought the three of us back here; father had already left for Amman. Tulkarm was occupied by then and our house, like many here, had been looted: rings and jewelry, our radio and phonographs, all small items that could be carried easily. Our uncle Uthman, the doctor, was arrested along with some other men in the town. They were suspected members or sympathizers of the commandos. We were terribly worried for them because the military commander here said he knew nothing of their case and we thought they may have been killed. We heard nothing of them for several weeks, until the middle of August, when they were released. They had been beaten to make them confess their connection with the commandos. I guess the Israelis could get nothing out of them; we were so happy to see uncle again. I wish they would let mother and father come back too; we are very frightened alone without them, although my cousin sleeps here at night to protect us."

The doctor himself entered a few moments later. He told me that the Israelis had gone through the files in the local police station as soon as they took Tulkarm. From the files they learned that several of the leading citizens were known to have had long-standing feelings against King Hussein. "In their minds that was sufficient to connect us with Fateh," he said, adding quietly, "in my mind the beatings they gave us are sufficient reason for me to want to join the resistance." He had a wife and family to consider but his expression of sympathy for Fateh was the measure of his bitterness against the Israelis. I found it hard to imagine this bespectacled, middle-aged gentleman with a machine gun in his hands.

None of us in the house was aware of it at the moment, but the resistance had already begun. Incidents in Gaza... An Arab in Hebron given ten years in prison for possession of a rifle and a sword... General strike called in Jerusalem... Arab commandos strike kibbutz... Israeli public opinion outraged at death of infant... And so it went.

Nablus, the largest town on the West Bank, was seething with discontent. Even under the British Mandate, Nablus had been the center of nationalist dissent. Teachers and students joined in a strike to protest the replacement of their school books with the "expurgated" Israeli versions. The mayor of Nablus told me that the city's prisons held nearly 400 detainees charged with a variety of political acts against the military regime. They had not yet been brought to trial. The Israeli military governor threatened long prison terms and heavy fines for any person who attempted to influence public opinion in any way. There were continual arrests and when weapons were discovered in a house it was immediately dynamited. On the day I saw the mayor in his office the news had just been received of eight high-school students who had been killed by an Israeli patrol while trying to slip across the Jordan River. They were unarmed, and apparently "on leave" from their school in Amman to see their families. The military governor listed them as Fateh agents.

Ramallah, a beautiful little town a few kilometers north of Jerusalem, was quiet when I passed through. It was here some weeks later that a crowd of 300 girls sat in the compound of their school chanting slogans such as "Palestine is our country" and "Long live Fateh." Steel-helmeted soldiers, armed with guns and clubs, then entered the compound swinging their weapons in every direction. According to the headmistress "the soldiers came tearing into the buildings. They clubbed anyone they saw. I saw my teachers being held by two soldiers and beaten by a third. Some of them had not been demonstrating but were attending classes peacefully with their students." The *London Observer*'s Gavin Young reported the incident at the time: "I saw girls of fifteen or less who had evidently been struck several times. One young teacher, covered with bruises and with a severe swelling on her forehead, was in bed unable to move. Other girls had multiple bruises. All told the same story of a wild charge by Israeli soldiers."

In al-Bireh, a small town next door to Ramallah, elderly women received the same treatment when they demonstrated against the rumored arrest of their mayor.

I left the West Bank and Israel and flew to the Lebanese capital of Beirut via Cyprus, the only means of commuting between hostile centers in this part of the world. I had left behind two different worlds where the memory of war was vivid in one and the traces of it visible everywhere in the other. Tel Aviv's was an atmosphere of fragrant exhilaration. Victory was sweet and everyone savored it to the full. Book shops were replete with accounts in pictures and words of "The Shortest War" or the "Miracle in the Desert." Eye-patched dolls of Moshe Dayan were on sale; plaques and pennants commemorated the martyrs of the war; others commemorated the reunification of Jerusalem after 2,000 years, forgetting, of course, that it had not been divided until 1948. A documentary film of the Six Day War was playing to audiences who cheered lustily whenever their generals appeared on the screen. The other world, the West Bank, seemed typified by the burnt-out shells of Jordanian tanks scattered by the wayside with Israeli tourists being photographed atop the silent machines. Jerusalem was somewhere in between. The capture of the Old City was being re-created for the movie cameras. Israeli tanks with guns blazing blanks and troops brandishing machine guns moved past the YMCA as a small group of Jerusalem Arabs stood watching silently.

Beirut was another world altogether. It had witnessed neither victory nor defeat. Lebanon stayed out of the June war proclaiming its traditional policy of non-involvement in the Arab-Israeli conflict and its neutrality in inter-Arab affairs. The nightclubs, discotheques and casinos buzzed with activity. Fashions were the latest Rome, Paris and London had to offer. Beirut banks were the private treasure houses of the oil rich

sheikhs of the Persian Gulf, Kuwait and Saudi Arabia. Legitimate
theaters entertained sophisticated audiences with Molière, Brecht
and Beckett. Art galleries had their appreciative buyers.

Beirut was all this and more. Yet it suffers a deep split in
personality. Not far away from this affluence were Palestinian
refugee camps, five of which lay on the outskirts of the city.
Beneath the surface of a dolce vita existence may be found the
intense political activity of various Palestinian organizations
which have their headquarters or branch offices in this capital.
A single room or two in an office building closets persons single-
mindedly devoted to the cause of revolution just as a bar or
cafe caters to those dedicated to a life of hedonism.

By means of an introduction through a lawyer acquaintance, I
was able to meet members of the political executive of the
Palestine Liberation Organization. The first thing I wanted to
know was where they stood on the question of their leader,
Ahmad Shukayri, who had made the most horrendous declarations
before the Six Day War about exterminating Israelis or shipping
them back to their countries of origin. Shukayri lived in a
magnificent villa high on a mountainside overlooking Beirut and
the Mediterranean, which struck me as somewhat at odds with
his role as head of a "revolutionary" army.

"Don't you think that Shukayri's declarations severely damaged
the morality of your cause? Is he representative of what Palestinians want and think?" My questions created an embarrassed
silence. Their answers were evasive or non-committal and we
shifted to other topics. Later, as the lawyer accompanied me
from his office to the corridor, he said: "You put them on the
spot about Shukayri. The P.L.O. is divided over what should be
done with him. I personally think the man is a dangerous
fanatic who has harmed our cause a great deal. He won't last
long." The lawyer, who did not want me to use his name, was
right. Shukayri was ousted a few weeks later. And with Shukayri
went Egyptian control of the Organization which, since 1964,
had been used to dominate the Palestinians rather than serve
their revolutionary interests. The P.L.O. is now under the wing
of Fateh, with Yassir Arafat as chairman of its executive.

That same day I went to see a leader of Fateh, known as Abu
Zuhayr, a highly competent engineer who had his own consulting

business and taught at the American University of Beirut. Originally from Gaza, his family had lost all their property in Palestine after the creation of Israel. But he symbolized hope for beleaguered Palestinians.

In contrast to others, Abu Zuhayr took a surprisingly cheerful view of the latest Arab defeat. "For us, the fifth of June is not a day of mourning, but a day of hope. Now, after twenty years, we are free to take a hand in guiding our own destiny. The time has come for the Palestinian masses to organize and take the struggle into their own hands. Only then will our voice as a people be heard. Until today we have been regarded as refugees, or simply United Nations statistics. The word refugee no longer exists for us. We are a nation of men, women and children, the Palestinian people who join the struggle to regain our roots in our homeland." Abu Zuhayr was under no illusions that the obstacles before them were easy or that liberation would be achieved tomorrow. He said: "For us, the Palestine Revolution is an imperative."

The first Christmas of the occupation came with lead-gray skies settling over the country. The drizzle, icy winds and near freezing temperatures harmonized with the sullen mood of the majority of the Palestinian population. A first snow had fallen in Galilee to brighten an otherwise somber landscape. Israeli soldiers built snowmen and fought pitched battles among themselves with snowballs. For the moment, the still tiny Fateh was the farthest thing from their minds. At the pilgrimage sites other security forces waited tensely for the Christmas celebrations to end. Disturbances had been threatened but the day passed without incident. On Cyprus a lonely man prepared to leave for Jerusalem on his mission of peace for the United Nations. Gunnar Jarring's mission was a hopeless and thankless task, traveling to and fro between the Arab capitals and Israel, striving patiently to find some way out of the deadly political impasse. Six months after the June war the prospects for peace were no better than the prospects for war.

In January of the new year, 1968, Fateh issued its first communiqué to the world press. "The Palestine Problem," it stated, "is essentially the problem of an entire people, the Arabs of

Palestine, uprooted and expelled from their homeland in order
to permit the establishment of Israel."

There were widespread misconceptions concerning the nature
of the Palestinian liberation movement which the communiqué
attempted to clarify. Fateh, it said, recognizes the failure of the
United Nations to resolve the conflict as well as the failure of their
own people, through the P.L.O., to further the cause of the
liberation of the homeland. Now, however, under different
circumstances and face-to-face with the Israeli occupier, the
Palestinian struggle has entered a new phase of popular resistance
of the masses. Arab citizens of Israel, inhabitants of the occupied
West Bank, the refugees, and Palestinians throughout the Arab
world will join the struggle, since it involves the fate of the
nation as a whole. The first stage of the revolution must accomplish
the mobilization of Palestinians everywhere to the cause of
liberation.

"Fateh wishes to point out, however, that its operations —
which today enjoy the support of the entire Palestinian people —
are in no way aimed at the Jewish people as such with whom they
lived in harmony in the past for so many centuries. *Nor does
it intend 'to push the Jews into the sea'*. Fateh is aimed solely at
the Zionist-military-fascist regime which has usurped our homeland
and expelled and repressed our two million people, condemning
them to a life of destitution and misery." Liberation in the eyes
of Fateh, does not mean the destruction of a people and
does not pose a threat to the existence of a society of individuals.
The Palestinians' challenge is directed at Israel's ideology of
exclusiveness, which insists on a particular ethnic-religious
identity for normal participation in its society.

"Fateh," the communiqué stated, "also wishes to correct once
and for all the Zionist insinuation that this 'terrorist' movement
is inspired and directed from the outside by such countries as
Syria, Jordan, Algeria or Egypt. Under the conditions existing in
the Middle East today, no such foreign-imposed 'movement' could
long survive for it would soon be rejected by the people. On the
other hand, the Palestinian People's Liberation Movement has
arisen out of their desperate frustration and deep aspirations for
liberty, justice and dignity in their own homeland."

Those who have suffered most from the existence of Israel are the Palestinians and it is they who are today taking their destiny into their own hands. Courage and armed struggle will restore their lost dignity. The Palestinian Revolution seeks to create a a new secular order and the vision of the future is that of the day when "the flag of Palestine is hoisted over their freed, democratic, peaceful land, a new era will begin in which the Palestinian Jews will again live in harmony side by side with the original owners of the land, the Arab Palestinians."

Fateh decries what it calls "Zionist hypocrisy," namely, the demand that Palestinians assimilate into the surrounding Arab countries. The narrow nationalist view of the Zionists rejects assimilation for the Jewish people, yet it urges this solution upon the Palestinians.

The guiding principle of Fateh, therefore, is armed struggle as the basis of revolutionary action. This stems from the failure of the Palestinian appeal for justice. Deeds, not words, must mold the course of events, and armed struggle will awaken the revolutionary consciousness of the masses. A second principle is that Palestinian liberation must be conducted by Palestinians themselves in order to maintain the focus upon the original character of the conflict which is Palestinian versus Zionist and not Arab against Israeli or, as many western commentators have distorted it, Arab versus Jew. As a consequence of these principles, Fateh has consistently eschewed the adoption of a rigid ideological posture. The Palestinian Liberation Movement should not identify itself with any one political ideology or regime but rather concentrate on the central goal of freeing the homeland.

From its revolutionary philosophy, Fateh has derived certain strengths. One is flexibility which is also a key to its phenomenal success. Flexibility in its relations with the Arab governments, since Fateh claims not to want to become involved in "side issues" such as the internal affairs of these governments. Flexibility, too, in its relations with other resistance groups, since it claims to be doctrinally neutral. This is not to say that tension is absent for, as in the cases of Jordan and Lebanon, tension has erupted into clashes with government forces.

King Hussein of Jordan has not known a day's (or night's, for that matter) rest since the June war. With the influx of the new refugees from the West Bank, King Hussein's truncated kingdom is overwhelmingly Palestinian in population. The newest political force in the country is now the total commando organization. The king has the qualified support of the army, the Bedouin chiefs and, of course, the royal household. His own position on the guerilla organizations has ranged from open denunciation to grudging approval. Hussein has denied that he is a prisoner of the commandos or that he has any formal relationship with them. The Jordanian Government has repeatedly acknowledged its adherence to the November resolution of the Security Council but the king has warned both Washington and Whitehall that if no other alternative is left to him he will have to throw in his lot with the commandos.

The United States, through its embassy in Amman and through CIA agents (who "infest this country" according to Fateh), has done everything possible to keep Hussein on his throne. It is believed, for example, that the U.S. was behind Hussein's announcement (February, 1970) of restrictions on the stockpiling, carrying and use of arms, a move which automatically led to clashes between the commandos and Jordanian security forces, resulting in at least thirty dead. After several frantic meetings between the two sides, King Hussein stated that the restrictions were not aimed at the *fidayin* at all but were intended as a reminder of existing laws and regulations. "The measures were not expected to meet such misunderstanding and uproar," the king explained lamely. The restrictions were "frozen" and King Hussein continues to walk his tightrope, safe for the moment in the knowledge that as long as he does not fall Israel will not move into the rest of his kingdom, as she has promised to do in the event of a change of government inimical to her interests. The commandos knew this too, and were prepared, for the moment, to coexist with the king. The Civil War of September 1970, as we shall see, changed everything.

Lebanon presented a more complex picture. Over the years Lebanese governments have studiously avoided becoming embroiled in the Arab-Israeli conflict. Elements among the Christian population, especially the Maronites, have gone so far in times of crisis as to deny Lebanon's belonging to the Arab world. The Muslim half of the population, with the exception of the wealthy business-landowning Establishment, identifies closely with Arab developments in general. The mountainous southern part of Lebanon, from which Palestinian guerillas have launched attacks against Israel's Galilee region, is predominantly Muslim. There are also several Palestinian refugee camps in the south. Geography and a basically sympathetic population make the south, therefore, ideally suited to commando activities. For the same reasons, Lebanese security forces find it difficult to control or check Palestinian incursions into Israel.

A crisis of grave proportions erupted in October 1969. Lebanese security forces surrounded the refugee village of Magdal Bani Salim in the south and opened fire on it. An army spokesman later claimed this was in response to gunfire from "a band of armed men." The incident touched off riots and demonstrations in Sidon, Beirut and the northern Lebanese town of Tripoli which, for a few days, was in the hands of insurgents. An oil pipeline near the port of Sidon was blown up. Commandos and regulars of the Lebanese Army sniped at each other in several districts. At the American University of Beirut a pro-commando demonstration was addressed by Layla Khalid, the young commando girl who had hijacked a TWA jet to Damascus the previous August. Her second attempt with an El Al airliner in September 1970 was almost successful. The country became paralyzed by fear of another civil war like that of 1958. Peace was finally restored when the Lebanese commander in chief, General Bustani, met with a Fateh delegation in Cairo to hammer out an accord.

In the Cairo agreements, Fateh scored important military and diplomatic points. For a pledge to accept close supervision by the Lebanese authorities, the commandos secured free access along the "Arafat Trail" leading from Syria across the mountains into northern Israel. In one article of the secret agreement, the Lebanese acknowledged that the Palestinian armed struggle was beneficial to the interests of Lebanon. Palestinians argued that their revolution did not conflict with Lebanese sovereignty since they shared a common enemy. Moreover, they pointed out with some force the long-standing Lebanese fear that Israel covets the southern part of the country up to the Litani River, an area containing valuable water resources and fertile orchards. The Lebanese needed no reminding that the Zionists' own plan for the Jewish State presented to the Paris Peace Conference in 1919 included this very region.

These encounters with Arab governments have strengthened the guerilla movement inasmuch as they represent the failure of both Jordan and Lebanon to crush it in its formative stage, while at the same time being forced themselves to recognize the legitimacy of the Palestinian armed struggle.

Fateh has also to face another kind of challenge from within the ranks of the resistance movement. As the largest, best equipped and most popular of the ten commando groups which make up the Unified Command, Fateh has had to assume the lion's share of responsibility for the continuing healthy state of the whole movement. This requires money, supplies and arms and consequently, good working relations with various Arab governments. The leaders of Fateh are determined to be tactful but never subservient, and they will quickly lash out at whatever they believe to be unwarranted interference. While other groups do not take strong issue with Fateh's pragmatic approach to politics, they quarrel with some of the practical implications.

The quarrel is joined on ideological grounds just where Fateh has sought to elaborate a non-ideological revolutionary philosophy. The Popular Front led by George Habbesh and the Democratic Popular Front led by Nayif Hawatmeh are advocates of the non-Communist left. Their criticism of Fateh is that the Palestine Revolution should not be confined solely to Palestine (or Israel and the occupied territories) but should engulf all of Arab society. The struggle is not against Zionism alone, but also against "imperialism," the chief agent of which is the United States, and all "reactionary" Arab governments. The Popular Front and the DPF are suspicious of Fateh's "conservative" nature as it is rather strongly represented by elements of the middle class and the petty bourgeoisie. Only the presence of the peasants, the urban workers and the refugees can bring about a total transformation of a guerilla war into a people's war of liberation. Finally, Fateh is criticized for making armed struggle a fundamental strategic principle without giving equal weight to political and ideological structures.

Fateh replies to its critics. It insists that as long as Palestinians are fighting to liberate their homeland, ideological commitment is not a substitute for a broad national front. It justifies its own position on the left, saying: "Despite the many definitions of the left in general, one can say that all genuine leftist movements aim at bringing about an end to man's exploitation of man by rejecting static conditions and structures and modifying them by resistance or by struggle and revolt." Fateh claims to represent the largest class of Palestinians, those who are uprooted, displaced and oppressed. Professor Hisham Sharabi, in his work on the Palestinian guerillas, has commented on the effects of this debate: "Despite its pragmatism, Fateh has tended to give increasing attention to political organization and to develop more focused political positions. The transformation of the guerilla nucleus into a political organization was under way much earlier than anticipated."

This process of transformation is due in some measure to the Democratic Popular Front of Nayif Hawatmeh. Now in his thirties, Hawatmeh was born into a peasant family in Jordan's East Bank. Tall, moustached, almost awkward in appearance, he was sentenced to death in 1956 for his political activities in Jordan. He escaped and made his way via Syria and Lebanon to Iraq where, two years later, he spent some months in prison under General Qasim's regime. When the June war broke out he was in Aden where he had been helping the resistance against British rule.

Hawatmeh had been associated for a number of years with George Habbesh, a physician turned guerilla and present leader of the Popular Front. Over differences of temperament and tactics, Nayif Hawatmeh broke with Habbesh and formed the DPF in February 1969. Habbesh's program claimed to be the simple application of Israeli policies to the Israelis themselves: if they used napalm to kill civilians and employed collective punishment, then the guerillas were equally justified in attacking Israeli civilian and military targets. Hawatmeh, however, repudiated the Popular Front's more spectacular exploits such as plane hijackings and urban bombings as ill-serving the revolution.

The political education of DPF members includes serious study of the history and perspectives of the Palestine Problem, the social and historical contexts from which sprang the revolutionary works of Guevara, Castro, Mao Tse-tung and Giap, and an investigation of the processes of radical social transformation in Cuba or Vietnam or China together with an inquiry into the failure of such a process in Algeria. Each camp or village in which the DPF operates is controlled by a council of seven persons, four freely elected and three elected from a list submitted by the DPF leadership. This limited but basic exercise in democracy has brought peasants and workers in close touch with the planning and development of the revolution, and the example is catching on in other groups.

All the commando groups have their contingents of *ashbal* or "lion cubs," boys ranging in age from seven to fourteen. They are given intensive training in unarmed combat as well as in the use of the more sophisticated weapons and explosives. This is in addition to their regular schooling and political education.

Young girls, and women too, are playing an increasingly important role in the revolution. As teachers, nurses, welfare workers and couriers, almost all receive some training in handling automatic weapons. The Palestinian woman's inspiration is drawn directly from the exploits of her counterpart in the Algerian revolution against the French. By their prior example, the harmonization of the role of the Palestinian woman to the aims of the revolution is made easier, but there remain many traditional values which hinder a woman's full participation in armed combat.

"We must move slowly but surely," Abu Marwan, a Fateh leader says. "At the moment the women's training camps are segregated from the men's. Soon the idea will be accepted by our parents' generation that it is right for a woman to participate in her new role. We are trying to rebuild Palestinian society from the bottom to the top and many of our old ways are inadequate. Changes are occurring, though. Sometimes so quickly that they take us by surprise."

He recounted an incident from his own experience which had impressed this change on him. "The Arabs," he said, "take death very seriously. Women cry and weep and moan for days after a death in the family — even for one who may not be a close relative. Our women are professional mourners. You can imagine my apprehension when I had to break the news to a mother that her son had been killed in action. I tried to introduce the subject gently, and then I just blurted out the news. I waited for the outburst. Nothing. Not a tear, not even a wrinkle on her poor face. 'It is for our country,' she said to me. 'I know that we must sacrifice for our country to be free.' Our mothers are very possessive about their children, you know. I was deeply touched by her words."

While Israel clearly regards the Suez front as the most important in *its* war of attrition with the Arabs (attrition is not an Arab monopoly), it has so far officially dismissed the Palestinian resistance as mere nuisance value. It is true that guerilla casualties are high. This much is admitted by the commando groups, although a detailed breakdown has never been published. In addition, the Israeli intelligence network has broken many commando cells in the occupied territories. This has led to the capture of several hundred Palestinians. It has even been rumored that Arabic-speaking Israelis (Jews from Middle Eastern countries) have infiltrated the ranks of Fateh. The Palestinians do not enjoy the same advantage since Arab Israelis who speak Hebrew have never been given positions of responsibility in the Israeli Government. Nevertheless, recent figures indicate that more Arab Israelis were arrested during 1969 for "activities against the State" than in the whole previous decade. Not surprisingly, many are from among the educated, marking the degree of alienation from the State which the Arabs in Israel have been made to feel. The guerillas have earnestly tried to rectify their disadvantage by giving their trainees a basic knowledge of Hebrew. In the sense that Israelis and Palestinians "talk" to each other at all, it is in the form of two-way monologues. The Voice of Israel broadcasts daily in Arabic, the rejoinder coming from the Voice of Fateh in Hebrew.

The intelligence and propaganda wars aside, the effect of the Palestinian guerilla movement on Israel is particularly difficult to measure. Israeli sources, rather than Palestinian, are perhaps a better yardstick by which to judge. In August 1969, Israeli Army sources revealed that since the June war fully one third of all its military casualties had been inflicted by the "terrorists." During the same period only thirty-eight civilians were killed indicating that, as the guerilla groups themselves claimed, military targets have been the primary objectives. Writing in the Israeli daily *Ma'ariv*, General Narkis stated: "Things have reached such a point by now (June 1969) that people have to be continually injected with morale boosters in order to preserve their confidence in our military strength and prevent them from losing it altogether."

The policy of reprisal or retaliation, the so-called "morale booster," may prove the most deadly trap Israel has set for itself. Far from deterring the Palestinian guerillas, reprisals have, in one case at least, provided an invaluable "morale booster" to Israel's enemy. On March 18, 1968, an incident occurred which caused a sharp rise in tension between Israel and the commandos. A bus carrying vacationers struck a mine in the southern Negev near Beer-Ora on the road to Eilat. A doctor and a young man accompanying him were killed and twenty-eight persons injured, most of them children. The Popular Front claimed responsibility while Fateh actually condemned the incident. A deep sense of outrage ran through Israel and there were loud cries for instant reprisal. In the early morning of the 21st, tanks and other armor, aircraft and helicopters and about 15,000 troops of the Israeli Defense Force moved across the Jordan in a two-pronged attack. The major assault was against the village of Karameh while a smaller force attacked three spots south of the Dead Sea. The attack lasted twelve hours and when the Israeli forces had withdrawn, Karameh was totally destroyed, 150 "terrorists" had been killed and over 100 taken prisoner. Israel gave her losses as twenty-three dead and seventy wounded; one plane and six tanks were destroyed. Observers believed, however, that the losses were probably heavier.

The Chief of Staff, Major General Bar-Lev announced that "ours was a clear and well-defined objective — to hit and destroy the terrorist elements and their bases. This was achieved." Later he said that the back of Fateh had been broken. The political objective of the attack was intended as a warning to King Hussein that Israel would not tolerate his support of the commandos. As events were to show, however, Israel miscalculated on both counts.

Israel had not delivered the knock-out blow. Commando operations, in fact, increased. In the one month period prior to the Karameh attack, thirty-seven acts of sabotage were committed. From mid-August to mid-September, 103 guerilla raids took place. Exactly one year later, in August 1969, the number of guerilla operations had increased to 480 for the month. Karameh was a turning point. Recruits flocked to the commando camps from all over the Arab world. This was gratifying, but nevertheless a mixed blessing. Qualified instructors were at a premium and as the new recruits kept coming, the quality of their training declined. This situation was rectified after some months, but not before it was reported that during this period some 50 percent of the commando deaths had occurred in training, mainly as a result of poor medical facilities and lack of supplies.

Another Israeli military analyst, Elie Landau, has observed that "the fighting with Fateh goes on violently every day. This is never mentioned in the news. Despite severe casualties, the guerillas keep mounting operations as though nothing has happened." The Palestinians, of course, count heavily on the psychological impact of their raids. A further example was the thirty-six-hour invasion of the Arkoub area of southern Lebanon by Israel in May 1970. It was designed as a "surgical operation" to uncover and wipe out the guerilla bases near the Mount Hermon sanctuary. Israeli army officials called the operation a complete success. The very next day rockets were again crashing into the Israeli towns near the border. The guerillas had made their point.

The invasion, however, had a second message addressed to the Lebanese Government. Lebanese Prime Minister Rashid Karameh had publicly acknowledged that there were two sides in Lebanon, one saying that commando action should be carried out from Lebanon whatever the consequences, the other opposing this view. "No government," he said, "can take either view without splitting the country." This would appear to be the situation the Israelis intended to exploit by their invasion. It may mark a new stage in Israeli strategy against the Palestinians by attempting to force an open split between the governments of Lebanon or Jordan and the guerillas. Indications are, however, that the strategy will only prolong the stalemate.

Epilogue

The summer of 1970 opened a new chapter in the Palestinian story. Jordan was the center of the action, but the eye of the hurricane was Amman itself. The capital, like ancient Rome, huddles around seven hills. On one hill King Hussein has situated one of his palaces. Opposite the palace, on one of the largest hills in Amman, lies the Wahdat refugee camp, known locally as the Republic of Palestine. The camp contains 70,000 inhabitants and all the commando groups have either offices or centers inside the grounds. Once inside the "Republic" a person is entirely free of Jordanian governmental control. The camp and the royal palace facing it symbolize the dual authority existing within the country as a whole. As the summer began, the two sides, Palestinian commandos and the king, were being relentlessly drawn toward a showdown.

Clashes between the army and the commandos had become frequent. Each time, a cease-fire of sorts was arranged like a makeshift dressing over a festering wound. In June, bitter fighting left 1,000 dead on both sides. King Hussein knew his sovereignty was compromised and that sooner or later he must crack down hard on the commando organizations. He opted for sooner rather than later as references to the Palestinian "terrorists" began to appear in the government press, radio and television. The change in nomiclature was the danger signal to the commandos.

Yassir Arafat worked hard to stave off a head-on collision. At this time he looked tired and drawn after the weeks of tension. Dark glasses concealed his eyes, but his voice betrayed the real anxiety which he felt. The warmth of the smile which he managed on occasion could not dispel the barrenness of the room which served as his momentary headquarters. It was here in Amman that Arafat said that it would be tragic for one Arab to spill the blood of another. "And to be quite frank about the situation," he continued, "although we are confident we will not lose if it comes to a direct and decisive confrontation with the king's army, we cannot be sure we will win; fighting would only result in stalemate." Arafat, like other commando leaders

I was able to reach, was deeply suspicious of the generals
around King Hussein although they maintained a certain
grudging respect for the monarch himself. Two generals in
particular became the target of attack since they were close
relatives of King Hussein, his cousin Major General Sherif
Zayd ben Shaker and his uncle Major General Nasser ben Jamil.
In a token gesture to appease the commandos, the king dismissed
his two relatives following the four days of fighting in June.
The real power in the army, however, lay in other hands. The
commandos accepted the king's gesture and continued to wait and
watch.

Late in July a political bombshell was thrown at the Palestinians: Egypt's President Gamal Abdel Nasser, recently returned
from three weeks of talks with Russian leaders in Moscow,
announced before the assembly of the Arab Socialist Union that
Egypt was accepting the American peace proposals as set forth
by Secretary of State William Rogers. The Israeli cabinet
which had also been mulling over the plan was taken aback by
Nasser's sudden move. The Palestinians were thunderstruck.

There was nothing new in the Rogers' plan. Basically, it
was a reiteration of the principles embodied in the Security
Council resolution of November 1967. What had changed prior
to President Nasser's death in late September was his apparent
determination to bring about a political settlement with Israel
and consequently recognition of the Jewish State. There were
compelling reasons for which Egypt agreed to the ninety-day
cease-fire period as a prelude to negotiations. Each missile site
constructed in the Suez Canal area cost upward of 500
lives of workmen and soldiers owing to saturation bombing
by the Israeli Air Force. Moreover, Egypt's main supporter,
Russia, was pushing Nasser to give the American plan a chance.
Direct confrontation between the two super powers was always
a distinct possibility which both Moscow and Washington
wanted to avoid.

President Nasser remained distrustful of American intentions
to the end. He knew that, while Washington had refused
Israel's request for a further 125 Phantom and Skyhawk jets,
it was prepared to replace all Israeli military losses and further to
prop up the Israeli economy to the tune of 100 million dollars.

And so, to a secret session of the National Congress on July 25, Nasser explained that his main motive for accepting the peace plan and cease-fire was to expose the Americans. "We do not trust Washington," he said, "but circumstances force us to try them. I assure you that we are still in the midst of a battle." Nasser was prepared to play the political game although perhaps at heart he was convinced it would come to nothing. The American peace initiative would be put to the test. President Nixon, early in July, had accused Egypt and Syria of extremism and of trying to throw Israel into the sea. Nasser countered by saying it was Israel which wanted to push the Arabs into the desert.

As Nasser did not trust Washington, the Palestinian commando groups took a second look at their champion in Cairo. The Egyptian president had previously been immune to public attacks on his policy by Palestinians, most of whom regarded him as the most faithful Arab leader. However, the day after Nasser's announcement of his acceptance of the Rogers Plan, the commando radio stations based in Cairo opened a verbal barrage against the president. Stung by this vehement opposition, Nasser had the radio broadcasts silenced. The Palestinians' sense of despair and isolation was frankly expressed by a commando leader in Beirut: "We are like the victim of a rape attempt; she knows she cannot win but she puts up a fight to show her decency." Palestinians had little chance of winning a war of words with Nasser but felt they had no choice but to fight.

King Hussein was eager to follow President Nasser's lead and accept the American peace initiative. He too realized that his acceptance would set light to a very short fuse. Finally, the king stated that his government would accept whatever Cairo accepted and reject whatever Cairo rejected. It was not a Solomonian judgment and the fuse began to burn.

Meanwhile, within the ranks of the commando movement, dissension broke out. Two minor groups urged patience with President Nasser, in order to give him time to exhaust the options of what they regarded as the president's tactical maneuver. The leaders of these two factions, Dr. Issam Sartawi and Ahmad Zaarour, argued that the peace plan would never work since the United States would not force Israel to withdraw from major portions of the occupied territories. Other commando groups, such as Dr. George Habbesh's Popular Front, maintained that the revolution could not encourage any peace proposal whose success would liquidate the Palestinian cause. Each side appealed to the logic of its position while Fateh once again assumed the role of mediator. From the heated discussions inside the Central Committee there emerged a compromise arrangement which was manifested in a silent demonstration of Palestinians from the Husseini mosque in central Amman to the headquarters of the Armed Struggle Command. There, Yassir Arafat reiterated the pledge of the revolution to liberate their homeland. But in rejecting the American proposals he avoided reference to those countries which supported them.

The specter which haunted Palestinians at this moment was of a wholesale sellout by Egypt. This could lead to other Arab governments pursuing a course defined by their own narrow national interests rather than by broader Arab interests of which the Palestine Problem was an integral part. Palestinians feared not so much a formal peace treaty with Israel, as the possible establishment of a "Palestinian State." This latter prospect might soothe the official Egyptian conscience as having done its best for the Palestinians. Such a plan, however, would involve two dangers: the first being the certain continuance of violence stemming from Egypt's by-passing the fundamental Palestinian right to participate in any final solution, and the second being that any proposed Palestinian state would, in reality, become nothing more than a simple Israeli colony.

Reflecting the general atmosphere of uncertainty, Fateh dispatched a high ranking official to Communist China, North Korea and North Vietnam with messages from Yassir Arafat concerning the current situation. The object of the trip was to secure a clear promise from the Chinese to maintain the flow of arms and ammunition to the revolution as well as to continue the training of Palestinian guerillas. (Shortly thereafter, Prime Minister Golda Meir went to Washington on a similar mission.) Palestinians were not discounting the possibility that the Arab countries and the Soviet Union might cut off the arms supplies should peace negotiations move ahead. Other delegations were sent to all Arab capitals to explain the commandos' position in the face of growing evidence that the intelligence networks of Jordan and Lebanon were combining (with or without the encouragement of Egypt which was uncertain) against the movement. Syria and Iraq gave their "unqualified" support to the revolution, a gesture which was soon put to the test.

Toward the end of August the Palestine National Congress met at Wahdat Camp in Amman. The Congress broadly represents the Palestinian people including both commando and civilian groups. The resolutions of the Congress again attacked the peace proposals but refrained from condemning either Cairo or Amman for accepting them. Despite this political restraint, continuing clashes between the commandos and the special forces of the king's army heightened the tension in Amman and increased the expectancy of a showdown. On both sides the strain had a telling effect as discipline collapsed. Someone attempted to assassinate King Hussein on his way to the airport to welcome his daughter. Army leaders took this as their cue to pressure the king into a decisive move against the commandos.

Then Dr. George Habbesh's Popular Front for the Liberation of Palestine stunned the world with its multiple skyjackings. Four planes were successfully plucked out of the skies, three of which were taken to a disused airstrip in the Jordan Desert. The fourth, a Pan-Am 747 jumbo jet was flown to Cairo where it was blown up, a symbolic protest to President Nasser for accepting the American peace proposals. The passengers of the remaining aircraft were held hostage for the return of commandos serving various sentences in Swiss and West German jails.

World reaction to the skyjackings was instant, unanimous and expected. The hard line adopted by Great Britain and the United States soon seemed impractical as West Germany and Switzerland were more anxious to secure the safe release of their own nationals than to keep Palestinian commandos in their jails. Reports from the first group of freed hostages revealed that they had all been correctly treated while some declared publicly that despite their ordeal they had suddenly, albeit unwillingly, acquired some insight into the Palestinian struggle.

Although Fateh denounced the skyjackings as counterproductive to the revolution, there is little doubt that the exploit was a

warmly-welcomed boost to the majority of Palestinians if not
Arabs in general. The skyjackings were applauded enthusiasti-
cally, especially among poorer Palestinians where the Popular
Front draws much of its support. The Front, which has suffered
chronic financial problems, might find itself better off in
the future; their leaders claimed that the most difficult part of
the entire skyjacking operation was getting enough money to
buy the airline tickets!

Whatever the skyjackings did for Palestinian morale, they
did nothing to improve the situation in Jordan. The king was
acutely embarrassed by the events since he appeared quite
powerless to prevent the hostages being held on Jordanian soil.
The confusion created in the capital by these skyjackings, however,
provided a useful diversion for the course of action the king
had now determined to follow: the annihilation of the Palestinian
commando movement.

Army forces struck against towns and villages south of the
capital catching the commandos off guard. In Ma'an, Karak,
Shobak, Tafileh and Suwaileh, the Bedouin and special forces
began attacking commando offices and killed whomever they
found inside. In Irbed, the second largest Jordanian town, and
in Zarka a sympathetic population solidly backed the commandos
and the government troops were driven off. However, not before
a commando base just outside Irbed had been wiped out by
heavy artillery and rocket fire. It was this incident which
caused General Mashhour Hadditha, a supporter of the
commandos, to tender his resignation as army commander.
In his resignation, Hadditha accused the commander of the
responsible army unit of perpetrating a senseless massacre
which equaled that of My Lai. Then, on September 16, King
Hussein replaced his civilian government by a military government.
The cabinet comprised five brigadiers, a major general, a colonel,
a lieutenant colonel and three majors. King Hussein's chief
aide, military governor and commander of the armed forces was
Field Marshall Habes Majali, a man whom the Bedouin troops
would obey implicitly.

Some of the king's advisors believed that royal authority
could be restored at the cost of only 200 or 300 lives. After

ten days of bloody civil war and estimates as high as 20,000 casualties, the kingdom was transformed into a death camp. One observer has called it an "urban" Vietnam. This description was not meant merely to symbolize the massive loss of civilian life, the shelling of defenseless refugees in their camps, the saturation shelling by government forces of public buildings and private homes in Amman, Irbid and Zarka. This "urban" Vietnam pitted the heavy armor and fire power supplied to the Jordanian Army by the United States against Palestinian commandos and guerillas supplied chiefly by China. Washington could scarcely conceal its approval of King Hussein's action. The alledged Syrian "invasion" of Jordan caused Washington to warn of this grave new threat to the lives of Americans in Jordan. It was common knowledge in the area that the Syrian "invasion" was launched by an armored brigade of the Palestine Liberation Army stationed in Syria. The Americans were clearly concerned with propping up Hussein at all costs, and were preparing the ground for their own invasion of Jordan to do so. No sooner had the cease-fire been agreed upon and Hussein safe again for the moment, than the American State Department announced that all of the king's losses would be replaced with new and better equipment. Yassir Arafat had once declared that Jordan would become the Hanoi of the Middle East. He was wrong. It is now the Saigon of the Middle East.

Jordan will never be the same again. The psychological gap between the Palestinians and the king has become an abyss. Moral support for the Palestinians came immediately from the late President Nasser in the form of a harshly worded telegram to King Hussein regarding the behavior of his army. Sudanese President Ja'far Numeiry delivered a stinging rebuke of the king at a press conference in Cairo. Numeiry detailed some of the wanton atrocities executed by the king's men. More decisive, perhaps, was the criticism of Tunisian Prime Minister Bahi Laghdam, a member of the Arab truce supervisory team sent to Jordan. Laghdam, a well-known moderate, charged the Jordanian Government with the premeditated attempt to liquidate Palestinian resistance. It had been widely acknowledged that Laghdam would not make exaggerated or irresponsible accusations against Hussein with whom Tunisia has long enjoyed good relations.

The Jordanian civil war was the latest and possibly the most critical phase in the Palestinians' long and bitter struggle for survival. Conflict and defeat have been their lot in this Unholy War. Now, more than at any previous moment, they feel isolated and very much on their own. This latest episode, too, seems to fit a single pattern basic to the Palestinians' story from the beginning. Their story is a story of denial. Great Britain denied independence to Palestine alone among the mandated territories in the post World War I period. Zionists denied the existence of a people and society in Palestine as they strove to transform it into a European Jewish enclave. Today, Arab governments which are incapable of successfully waging either war or peace on behalf of the Palestinians appear determined to deny them the only alternative of struggling on their own behalf. And yet, one inescapable fact remains. Palestinians themselves have refused to accept the fate designed and determined for them by others, whether Arab, Israeli or American.

Bibliography and Notes

The literature dealing with the history of modern Palestine and the Arab-Israeli conflict (or the Palestine Problem) is vast. It would be impossible to provide the reader with a complete list of books on these subjects, just as it would be impractical to cite all the material which the author read in preparing this book, much of which is not currently to be found in book shops, nor available in all public libraries. In the bibliographical material provided for each chapter the criteria of importance and availability have guided the author in his selection. The notes will give further sources but are intended chiefly to give the origin of quotations found in the text of the book.

Chapter One:

Arthur Hertzberg has written an excellent essay on the historical development of the Zionist ideology in the introduction to *The Zionist Idea,* New York (1966) which also contains excerpts from the writings of the major Zionist thinkers. The diplomatic side of the Zionist movement has been treated in a short but penetrating work by Alan R. Taylor, *Prelude to Israel,* New York (1959). *The Balfour Declaration* by Leonard Stein, London (1961) remains the most exhaustive exposition of this controversial document.

1. Hertzberg, *The Zionist Idea,* pp. 181-198, for the text of *Auto-Emancipation.*
2. *Ibid.,* pp. 200-230, for the text of *The Jewish State.*
3. Taylor, *Prelude to Israel,* p. 6.
4. *The Complete Diaries of Theodore Herzl,* ed. R. Patai, New York (1960) Vol. I, p. 88, entry for 12 June, 1895.
5. Quoted by Hans Kohn, "Zion and the Jewish National Idea," in *Menorah Journal,* (Autumn-Winter, 1958).
6. Quoted in Michael Ionides, *Divide and Lose: The Arab Revolt of 1955-1958,* London (1960).
7. Weizmann's own account of his activities can be found in his autobiography, *Trial and Error,* New York (1966).
8. Weizmann, *Trial and Error,* p. 149.
9. H.F. Frischwasser-Ra'anan, *Frontiers of a Nation,* London (1955), p. 80.
10. *Palestine: A Study of Jewish, Arab and British Policies,* published by the ESCO Foundation for Palestine, New Haven (1947), Vol. 1, pp. 88-89. See also J.M.N. Jeffries, *Palestine: The Reality,* London (1939), p. 129.
11. *Palestine: A Study of...,* Vol. 1, p. 91.
12. Weizmann, *Trial and Error,* p. 244.
13. *Palestine: A Study of...,* Vol. 1, p. 95.
14. Jeffries, *Palestine,* pp. 181-182.
15. Weizmann, *Trial and Error,* p. 207.
16. For a comment on Lord Balfour's personal position on the Balfour Declaration, see *Middle East Journal,* (Summer, 1968), pp. 340-345.
17. *Documents on British Foreign Policy, 1919-1939,* eds. Woodward and Butler, First Series, Vol. 4, (1956), document 242, p. 345.

Chapter Two:

Several excellent books have recently appeared which provide essential material for an understanding of the nineteenth century Middle East. The political history is treated in P.M. Holt's *Egypt and the Fertile Crescent, 1516-1922,* New York (1969). The first part of A.L. Tibawi's *A Modern History of Syria, including Lebanon and Palestine,* London (1969), contains additional details. A brilliant and lucid intellectual history, *Arabic Thought in the Liberal Age, 1798-1939,* by Albert Hourani, London (1962), contains an important chapter on Arab nationalism. For Arab views of Europe during the nineteenth century see Ibrahim Abu-Lughod's *Arab Rediscovery of Europe,* Princeton (1963).

Chapter Three:

The classic statement of the origins of the Arab nationalist movement and the relations between Britain and France and the Arabs during World War I is *The Arab Awakening* by George Antonius, New York (1965), who himself served in the Palestine Government under the British Mandate. The second part of A.L. Tibawi's *A Modern History of Syria...* (see above, Chapter 2) covers the same period in which the author has made good use of hitherto un-published documents of the British Foreign Office.

1. Albert Hourani, "The Decline of the West in the Middle East" in *The Modern Middle East,* ed. Richard Nolte, New York (1963), p. 39 and p. 41.

Chapter Four:

1. David Ben Gurion, *Rebirth and Destiny of Israel,* New York (1954), pp. 7-27.
2. Greater detail on the early relations between Arabs and Zionists will be found in two articles by Neville Mandel: "Turks, Arabs and Jewish Immigration into Palestine, 1882-1914" in *St. Antony's Papers,* No. 17, Oxford (1965); "Attempts at an Arab-Zionist Entente 1913-1914" in *Middle Eastern Studies,* Vol. 1, (1965), pp. 238-267.
3. Barnet Litvinoff, *The Road to Jerusalem,* London (1965), p. 132.
4. *Palestine: A Study of...* Vol. 1, p. 131.
5. Quoted in W.F. Boustany, *The Palestine Mandate Invalid and Impracticable,* Beirut (1936), p. 136.

Chapter Five:

Two works which may be consulted for the period of the Mandate as a whole are *Cross-Roads to Israel* by Christopher Sykes, New York (1968), and *The Seat of Pilate,* by John Marlowe, London (1959). Although Sykes' Zionist sympathies are clearly acknowledged, the book is very readable and quite well balanced. Very little has been written on the Palestinian position and viewpoints. One book has recently appeared which will help to fill this gap, *Palestine is my Country: The Story of Musa Alami,* by Geoffrey Furlonge, London (1969). A documentary history from the pre-Mandate period to the June war of 1967 has been published by Walter Laqueur, *The Israel-Arab Reader,* New York (1969).

1. *Palestine: A Study of...,* Vol. 1, pp. 261-62.
2. Hertzberg, *The Zionist Idea,* p. 65.
3. *Palestine: A Study of...,* Vol. 1, p. 265.
4. F.F. Andrews, *The Holy Land under Mandate,* 2 Vols., New York (1931), Vol. 2, p. 86.

5. *Commission on the Palestine Disturbances of August, 1929*, Cmd. 3530, p. 129.
6. Andrews, *The Holy Land...*, Vol. 2, pp. 206-210.
7. Cmd. 1540, October 1921, p. 57.
8. *Palestine: A Study of...*, Vol. 1, p. 272.
8a. *Ibid*, Vol. 2, pp. 619-621.
9. *Ibid*, Vol. 1, p. 159. See also Muhammad Asad, *The Road to Mecca*, London (1954), p. 94.
10. Arthur Koestler, *Thieves in the Night*, New York (1946), p. 38.
11. N. Bentwich and M. Kisch, *Brigadier Frederick Kisch*, London (1966), p. 98.
12. Hertzberg, *The Zionist Idea*, p. 616.
13. Albert Hyamson, *Palestine under the Mandate: 1920-1948*, London (1950), Chapter 6.
14. Nevill Barbour, *Nisi Dominus*, London (1946), p. 156.
15. As observed by the Zionists' own commission of experts, Andrews, *The Holy Land...*, Vol. 2, p. 147.
16. Marlowe, *The Seat of Pilate*, pp. 100-101.
17. Barbour, *Nisi Dominus*, p. 135.
18. A.L. Tibawi, *Arab Education in Palestine*, London (1956), p. 103.
19. *Ibid*, pp. 123-124. See also Hyamson, *Palestine...*, p. 48.

Chapter Six:

The most detailed study of the political history of the Mandate from 1936-1948 remains that of J.C. Hurewitz, *The Struggle for Palestine*, New York (1950). It contains an excellent bibliography.

1. The story of illegal Jewish immigration into Palestine is told by Jon and David Kimche in *The Secret Roads*, New York (1955), but it is, unfortunately, difficult to find.
2. Walid Khalidi, "Plan Dalet," *Middle East Forum*, Vol. 36, November, 1961. See also Ben Halpern, *The Idea of the Jewish State*, Cambridge, Mass., (1961), p. 44 for the views of Haim Arlosoroff.
3. Many of the details of the revolt have been taken from contemporary reports by the London *Times* correspondent in Palestine.
4. Hourani, "Decline of the West," (see above Chapter 3)
5. *Jewish Chronicle*, 13 May, 1938.

Chapter Seven:

1. Yehuda Bauer, "The Haganah, 1938-1946," *Middle Eastern Studies*, Vol. 2 (1966), pp. 182-210; see also Hurewitz, *The Struggle for Palestine*, pp. 93 and 109.
2. Arthur Koestler, *Promise and Fulfillment: Palestine 1917-1949*, New York (1949), p. 12.
3. Kimche, *Secret Roads*, p. 27.
4. *Ibid*, p. 54.
5. Hyamson, *Palestine...*, p. 150.
6. *Ibid*, pp. 67-69.
7. See the article by Y.S. Brenner, "The Stern Gang, 1940-1948" in *Middle Eastern Studies*, Vol. 2 (1966), pp. 2-30.
8. Richard P. Stevens, *American Zionism and U.S. Foreign Policy, 1942-1947*, New York (1962), especially Chapters 5 and 6.

Chapter Eight:

1. Netaniel Lorch, *The Edge of the Sword: Israel's War of Independence, 1947-1949*, New York (1961), p. 84.
2. *Ibid.*, p. 87.
3. Rony E. Gabbay, *A Political Study of the Arab-Jewish Conflict*, Paris (1959), pp. 76-77.
4. For more complete details, see Walid Khalidi's article, "Plan Dalet," *Middle East Forum*, Vol. 36, November 1961.
5. Walid Khalidi, "Why did the Palestinians Leave?" *Middle East Forum*, Vol. 34, July 1959, p. 22.
6. Walid Khalidi, "The Fall of Haifa," *Middle East Forum*, Vol. 34, December 1959, pp. 22-34. For an account which differs from that of Khalidi, see Jon and David Kimche, *Both Sides of the Hill*, London (1960), pp. 118-124. Prof. Khalidi's interpretation has not yet been successfully challenged.
7. *Ibid.*, p. 32.
8. Edgar O'Ballance, *The Arab-Israeli War, 1948*, New York (1957), p. 64.

Chapter Nine:

For this and subsequent chapters, the reader may wish to consult parts of the following works for greater detail on different aspects of our story. Erskine Childers, *The Road to Suez: A Study of Western-Arab Relations*, London (1962), tries to dispel some of the myths which Europeans (and North Americans) have of the Arabs and of themselves regarding their relations with the Arab world. A brilliant and penetrating study of the period from 1948 to the Six Day War is that of Maxime Rodinson, *Israel and the Arabs*, London (1968). *The Covenant and the Sword: Arab-Israeli Relations 1948-1956*, London (1962), by Earl Berger, deals with the establishment and failure of the armistice agreements. In his book *The Arab-Israeli Dilemma*, Syracuse (1968), Fred Khouri has covered the three Arab-Israeli wars making exhaustive use of United Nations documents. The Palestinians' fate after 1948 is dealt with by Don Peretz in his *Israel and the Palestine Arabs*, Washington (1958).

1. Musa Alami, "The Lesson of Palestine," *Middle East Journal*, Vol. 3 (1949), pp. 373-405.
2. Malcolm Kerr, *The Arab Cold War 1958-1967: A Study of Ideology in Politics*, 2nd ed. London (1967), pp. 150-51.
3. A.H. Abidi, *Jordan: A Political Study, 1948-1957*, London (1965), p. 50.
4. *Ibid.*, pp. 26-38.
5. United Nations press release, 11 February, 1957.

Chapter Ten:

In addition to Peretz' book mentioned above (Chapter 9), three other works, all with the same title, *The Arabs in Israel*, will provide the necessary background on the Arab-Israeli community. The first by Walter Schwartz London (1959) is well balanced and describes the impact on the Palestinians resulting from their sudden transformation to a minority. The second book by Jacob Landau, Oxford (1969), contains an excellent analysis of Arab voting patterns in Israel. The last book is by Sabri Jiryis, Beirut (1968), who is an Arab-Israeli. It contains penetrating and sometimes bitter criticisms of Israeli

Government policies concerning the Arab minority but it is very well documented and gives details not to be found elsewhere.

1. *Jewish Observer*, 9 November, 1956.
2. *Jewish Observer*, 16 November, 1956.
3. *Jerusalem Post*, weekly airmail edition for October 23, 1967.
4. Gabbay, *A Political Study...*, p. 153.
5. Peretz, *Israel and the Palestine Arabs*, p. 36.
6. *Ibid.*, p. 150.
7. Laqueur, *Reader*, pp. 162-63.
8. *Times* (London), 15 June, 1969.
9. *Le Monde*, 20 January, 1969.
10. Jiryis, *The Arabs in Israel*, p. 5.
11. *Ibid.*, p. 21.
12. *Ibid.*, p. 43.
13. *Ibid.*, p. 52.
14. *Ibid.*, p. 46.
15. *Ibid.*, pp. 92-118 for details from the court records.
16. *Ibid.*, p. 140.

Chapter Eleven:

In this and subsequent chapters dealing with events since June 1967, the author has relied upon a variety of sources from interviews and close observation of the day-to-day situation. The following books are given to provide the reader with further background and detail.

Hisham Sharabi, *Palestine and Israel: The Lethal Dilemma*, New York (1969)
_____, *Palestine Guerillas: Their Credibility and Effectiveness*, Washington (1970).
Ania Francos, *Les Palestiniens*, Paris (1968).
Gérard Chaliand, *La Résistance Palestinienne*, Paris (1970).
Y. Harkabi, *Fedayeen Action and Arab Strategy*, London (1968).

General Index

Lithographié au Canada par:
ATELIERS DES SOURDS (Montréal) Inc.
85 ouest, rue DeCASTELNAU - MONTRÉAL 327   6